Dead & Buried

in Sussex

incorporating

What the Vicar Saw

David Arscott

Published in 2007 by Pomegranate Press
Dolphin House, 51 St Nicholas Lane, Lewes, Susssex BN7 2JZ
website: www.pomegranate-press.co.uk

*Front cover photograph: Eighteenth century gravestone to
Mary Box at Ardingly (page 7)
Back cover: monument to circus proprietor Fred Ginnett at
the Extra-Mural Cemetery, Brighton (page 12)*

Dead & Buried in Susssex first published by S.B.Publications 1997
What the Vicar Saw first published by Pomegranate Press 1998

ISBN 978-0-954-89755-0

British Library Cataloguing-in-Publication Data
A cataologue record for this book is available from the British Library

for Warden Swinfen

Afflictions sore long time he bore
In tussling with my text.
Though this world's gains
                        are few, his pains
Should earn more in the next.

**Imposing sixteenth century memorial to Sir
Nicholas Pelham in St Michael's church,
Lewes (*see page 13*).**

Other books by the same author include:

A Sussex Kipling
Wunt be Druv
In Praise of Sussex
The Sussex Story
Living Sussex
Our Lewes
The Neat & Nippy Guide to Lewes
Brighton in the News
A Century of Brighton & Hove
A Century of Eastbourne
Eastbourne Past and Present
Horsham Past and Present
Amberley Castle
Chailey Heritage
Sussex Bedside Anthology
Sussex – the County in Colour
Sussex – a Colour Portrait
Sussex Privies
East Sussex Events
Curiosities of East Sussex
Curiosities of West Sussex
The Upstart Gardener
A Sussex Quiz Book
A Second Sussex Quiz Book
Hastings & the 1066 Country
Explore Sussex
The Sussex Gardens Book
The Sussex Millennium Book
Agelines
Tales from the Parish Pump

with Warden Swinfen:

Hidden Sussex
Hidden Sussex – the Towns
People of Hidden Sussex
Hidden Sussex Day by Day

People who find churchyards spooky and depressing places must wonder what it is that appeals to those of us who spend many a happy hour scrambling among lichen-spattered gravestones, for ever stooping to decipher their laconic, weather-worn inscriptions. Although we can certainly muster an impressive array of worthy reasons for our passion – invoking Gray's *Elegy* as an impeccable sanction for relishing each gallery of village Hampdens, little tyrants and inglorious Miltons who, cheek-by-jowl in their long home, have bequeathed us a vivid sense of their community's chequered history – honesty demands that we also admit an unscholarly delight in the curious and unexpected. While most epitaphs and memorials are dull affairs (and who are we to demand anything else of them?), the exceptional few can move us to laughter, admiration or tears.

This book, designed for like-minded collectors of commemorative wonders, makes no pretence of academic thoroughness, and it records the last Sussex resting places of the famous and influential only if they or their loved ones have devised some striking way of remembering them. A graveyard, as far as these pages are concerned, is a meritocracy in which immortality is certain only for those who, whether by accident or design, have left us something bold, imaginative or downright strange to gaze at.

Good taste is the ruination of potentially fascinating epitaphs, but it can hardly be avoided here. Although young children do make the occasional appearance, a whole section devoted to their deaths would have been unbearable in what is intended primarily as an entertainment. Similarly, although the twentieth century is certainly represented, I have tried to avoid details which might upset or offend close relatives.

Each passing year defaces the old stones, and some of the epitaphs recorded here are already legible only with diligence and a good light. The best, however, are perhaps yet to be written. A touch of individuality is still to be found in our graveyards, and I have left a small space at the end of the book by way of encouragement to my readers. After all, those of us who care about such things really ought to make sure that we have the very last word.

David Arscott

The earliest decipherable Sussex gravestone?

Although the wealthy had displayed their grand monuments inside our Sussex churches for centuries, it was only during the seventeenth century that wooden churchyard memorials gave way to stone.

This unusual concentrically lettered headstone to the family of Robert Buckland at St Michael's, Lewes, is dated 1631, but its style suggests that it may have been erected some years later.

ACKNOWLEDGEMENTS

Ferreting for epitaphs is a thoroughly enjoyable pastime, but I would never have found so many without a good deal of generously offered help.

Thanks, first, to Christine Payne of the Sussex Family History Group, and to her many members, most unknown to me, whose painstaking researches in our churchyards are gradually furnishing an exhaustive record of the county's epitaphs. (Volunteers are made most welcome, and your local library will give you the name of someone to contact should you wish to enlist.) Deciphering ancient, moss-covered lettering can be the very devil, and it has been a relief on occasion to rely on their labours. Warden Swinfen, good friend and fellow scribe, has kindly given time and thought to the text, much to its improvement. My thanks, too, to the following, as to those passing souls who, the length and breadth of the county, have pointed a floundering author in the right direction: Jean Allen, Robert Armstrong, Fred Avery, Clinton Bothwell, Mary Breeds, John Brown, Alan Burtenshaw, Fiona Dakers-Black, Norman Edwards, Pat Eves, Jack Finch, John Ford, Joyce Freeland, Christine Heather, Vida Herbison, David Holland, Ron Iden, Bob Lomas, Gwyn Mansfield, Joy Marten, Maire McQueeney, Ann Money, Iveagh Moon, Ann Nortcliff, George Osborne, Tony Payne, Janet Pennington, Derrick Randall, Keith Richardson, Dave Rowland, John Saunders, Adrian Scriven, John Trendell and Maurice Williams.

I have generally laid out the epitaphs in the form in which they appear, but restrictions of space have occasionally dictated otherwise. Punctuation is often random or non-existent on our gravestones, and this can be part of their charm, but where it is uncertain I have at times given the mason the benefit of the doubt in order to aid the reader's understanding.

CONTENTS

The *memento mori* theme is common on eighteenth century headstones. The skull and crossbones *(above)* at St John sub Castro, Lewes, is surmounted by two winged creatures and an hour-glass. At Westbourne *(right)*, several stones are carved with gaunt skeletons, some of them escaping from their coffins.

Death's hurdle race: cast-iron 'leaping boards' for the Medhurst family outside St Anne's, Lewes. Early graveyard memorials in this style were made of wood, and the oldest in England can be seen inside the church at Sidlesham.

HISTORY IN STONE

Imagine the sombre scene in a typical Sussex village three hundred years ago. A gaggle of mourners shuffles along behind the parish bier, on which the body of the dear departed lies trussed in a simple woollen shroud firmly tied at either end – the material ordained by a law of 1667 designed to bolster the wool trade.

They approach the churchyard, each section of its wooden fence maintained by a family of means, the stout posts carved with their initials. The party pauses for a while beneath the roofed lych-gate ('lych' from the Old English for 'corpse'), waiting for the parish priest who is required by the Prayer Book of 1549 to begin the funeral service here.

Inside the church, coffin stools have been provided to relieve the bearers' arm muscles, but since our dead man was among the local poor he is denied the dignity of a private box: his remains will be lowered into the ground in nothing more substantial than that shroud, and the spot will be marked, until it rots away, by at most a simple wooden board.

If it seems to its participants a timeless ceremony, a glance about them will reveal that change is under way. A new prosperity is spreading through the community, and several families who once would have shared this dead man's anonymity can now afford to raise squat stones to their loved ones. The churchyard has been used in the past for archery, bowls and other sports (in 1662 two Boxgrove men were accused of playing cricket during evensong), but clusters of memorials will soon render such profanities impossible.

The old parish bier can still be seen in the church tower at Bury, and there are coffin stools at Beddingham and in the General Baptist chapel at Billingshurst, but the most common evidence for the many centuries of burials in Sussex is the height of our churchyards. As Kenneth Lindley has famously remarked, six burials a year over 800 years will have packed as many as 4,800 bodies into the ground, often necessitating the excavating of a drainage ditch around the church itself. In one sense, at least, the dead have already risen.

Those family names on the fence ('church-marks') survive in a number of Wealden parishes, including Chiddingly, Lindfield and Cowfold, the latter's celebrated on a special board by the lych-gate. The most notable early wooden survival, however, is the grave marker to Thomas Greenwood at Sidlesham. This is a 'dead' or 'leaping' board – a pair of oak beams set between two posts across the grave and recording his details on both sides:

HERE LYETH THE BODY OF
THOMAS GREENWOOD
WHO DECEASED THE 6
DAY OF MAY ANNO DOM 1658.

Leaping boards are sometimes still made today – and there's a good collection of 19th century cast-iron examples *(facing page)* at St Anne's in Lewes – but this one is remarkable both for being the oldest of its kind anywhere in the country and for having led a charmed life. It was nobbled by an opportunistic carpenter to repair a door at Paddock Cottage in Church Lane, and it was only the vigilance of a later carpenter that rescued it for posterity – in a glass cabinet inside the church.

The very oldest decipherable stone markers in our Sussex churchyards (if we discount the doubtful Buckland memorial which is pictured on page 2) mimic their wooden predecessors in consisting of an inscribed bar between two supports – a conservatism common enough in the history of design. These are to be found at Bolney, the first dating from 1660. As the years pass, the Bolney stone 'leaping boards' become taller: other examples of this second stage can be seen in the same area at Ardingly and Chailey.

Our exploration of a typical Sussex burial ground begins to the south of the church since this is generally, though by no means exclusively, where the oldest stones are to be found. Newcomers to memorial-hunting will be surprised by the clarity of some of these ancient inscriptions, but the reason isn't hard to find. The stones are small and chunky, and the men who carved them – local builders for the most part, often of patchy literacy and with no specialist training – chiselled deep into them. Their handiwork has often survived much better than the finer lettering of their successors two centuries later.

What may seem shocking at first

Early gravestones, like this one to Thomas Watts and his sister Ann at Sidlesham, confront the horror of death without a trace of Christian piety.

encounter is the complete absence of Christian sentiment in the wording. The early stones usually record only the barest details of name, age and date of death, and although taller and slimmer memorials are introduced in the early eighteenth century, allowing longer inscriptions and some elaborate pictorial embellishments by a new, more skilful breed of monumental masons, the pitilessness of Death is an abiding theme. It stares at us from blank eye sockets. Joseph Palmer's

These ancient stone grave markers at Bolney take their form from the earlier wooden 'leaping boards'. The oldest of them, to John Hills, is dated 1660.

stone of 1732 at Arundel is typical of the period, with its grisly skull and crossbones above an utterly woebegone message:

By cruel death I am separated here
From those I lov'd, my wife and
children dear

Although a rediscovery of classical symbolism brought a rash of hour-glasses, scythes and chubby winged cherubs (many of them brightly painted when new), few masons seemed able to resist the excuse for showing the bone beneath the skin. The Resurrection may be good news, but at Westbourne *(page 4)* it's depicted horrifically, with determined skeletons climbing out of their coffins.

The earliest stone markers generally came in pairs, with the name and other details at the head and an epitaph at the foot, and until the nineteenth century the inscriptions would face outwards, a sensible arrangement making it unnecessary to trample over the graves in order to read them.

What has remained consistent is the east-west alignment of the graves, in common with the church building itself, although the shape of a site will sometimes dictate that the chancel in reality faces a symbolic, 'ecclesiastical' east.

The stone to Helena Bennett at Horsham *(above, right)* stands out precisely because it breaks this rule. She was a Muslim from the Middle East who became a Roman Catholic when she took an English husband. He later deserted her,

and the positioning of her gravestone (quite obviously no accident) perhaps served to settle the scores.

Mary Box's headstone of 1771 at Ardingly *(front cover)* shows a grim, skeletal Death thrusting a spear into its curvaceous victim while winged Time strides from the scene.

An exception to prove the rule. Graves lie east-west in a Christian churchyard, but not Helena Bennett's at Horsham.

The eighteenth century generally gives us the most striking, individualistic gravestones, enlivened by dramatic and imaginative scenes.

'Those unknown carvers,' wrote John Betjeman, lamenting a lost age of crafts-manship, 'are of the same race as produced the vigorous inn signs which were such a feature of England before the brewers ruined them with artiness and

Let me out! Mark Sharp's headstone at St John sub Castro church, Lewes, has a vigorous Resurrection scene, his body rising from a boat-like coffin *(bottom right of the picture)*, summoned by a lusty trumpet blast from one of the angelic host. Sharp, as his footstone reveals *(p 42)* was a local carpenter.

standardization. They belong to the world of wheelwrights and wagon-makers, and they had their local styles.'

These men, obviously relishing their opportunity, have yet to be tamed by any attempt to impose a uniform good taste on their work. Apart from their vigorous Resurrections and Last Judgements, they sometimes create graphic, detailed death scenes which would shock us if they were carved today. For the victim of a road crash to be shown trapped under the wheels of his car would surely strike us as macabre, but poor Charles Cook lies lifeless under a felled tree *(p 22)*, young Ann Rusbridger is crushed by a barrel *(p 22)* and Thomas Barrow is flung into the sea from his sloop *(p 29)*.

The quirky verses which adorn many of these stones are sometimes original, worked up by the local schoolmaster or the vicar, but others are found (with slight variations) all over the country. Probably the most widespread of them all is this stoical quatrain, commonplace in Sussex:

Afflictions sore long time I bore
Physicians were in vain,
Till God did please Death should me seize
And ease me of my pain.

By the early nineteenth century much of the verve and originality has gone, as the monumental masons turn increasingly to copy-books for their inspiration. Our churchyard stroll will reveal many examples of fine italic and highly decorated lettering, not to speak of a scattering of Adam-style draped urns and drooping foliage, but the skill is usually practised at the expense of wit and daring. We hope against hope to be surprised.

There's no promise of the hereafter for Thomas Young at Hartfield, only a grim skull and crossbones and a moral: 'Death is the painful way that all Must Tread.'

And yet we *can* still be surprised in parts of East Sussex, where the pretty terracotta plaques of Jonathan Harmer (1762-1849) offer us a last, and distinctive, one-man display before the age of mass production sets in. The son of a Heathfield stonemason, Harmer specialised in these dainty bas-reliefs, devising a secret technique nobody else was able to copy. They can be seen at more than a dozen churches in the east of the county, usually set into headstones although occasionally incorporated in monuments inside the church.

Cast either in red clay from the Heathfield area or in a paler imported clay, they were offered in a relatively narrow range of designs, which included baskets of fruit and flowers, ornamental vases and the inevitable winged cherubs. A more showy classical motif was the figure of Charity suckling three children. The plaques are unmistakable, and most of them carry Harmer's name for good measure.

Like the kiln-fired 'artificial' stoneware named after its inventor, Eleanor Coade, and used for a number of Sussex monuments, Harmer's plaques enabled the quite-well-off to give their memorials a touch of class without breaking the bank. Cast iron crosses were cheaper still. Crosses of any sort were rare before the second half of the nineteenth century, smacking of popery, but at a time when the 'smells and bells' rituals of High Anglicanism were taking hold in our parish churches, they began to spread like a rash across churchyards which were often becoming so full (practically everyone could afford a memorial now) that overspill plots had to be found in the villages, new cemeteries on the edges of the towns.

Jonathan Harmer terracotta plaques at Mayfield. He devised these attractive, and surprisingly hard-wearing, gravestone ornaments after taking over the family business in 1799, and they can be found in churchyards all over the Heathfield area.

The Victorians bequeathed us great swathes of unimaginative memorials. Machine-made lettering was inserted into glistening headstones fashioned from imported white marble, and the epitaphs themselves became similarly standardised and unoriginal, whether Shakespearian ('Fear no more the heat o' the sun') or, much more often, impeccably Christian in sentiment: 'Gathered in', Gone before', 'Asleep in Jesus' and the rest. A depressing heaviness sets in. 'Increasingly, grave plots came to be regarded as private property,' finds John Roles, 'emphasised by the appearance of railings, fences and kerbs surrounding them.'

Whatever their aesthetic quality, we should be thankful to our churchyards for their valuable, if patchy, record of their community's past – a history in stone which tells of families great and humble, epidemics and sudden tragedies, trades and occupations, heroism and the harvests of war. Recording the fading epitaphs before they are lost for ever is historically important as well as entertaining.

That said, two of our most interesting burial plots, both very small, have no individual headstones at all. In the churchyard at Westham four boulders half buried in the earth in the shape of a cross mark the site of a communal grave dug in 1666 for victims of the plague. And at Twineham four stones offer similar mute testimony (though a separate stone, pictured right, now gives what we might call the bare bones of the story) to the decidedly unusual burial in this Anglican churchyard of several dozen Quakers between 1694 and 1732.

This is a strange tale. The Quakers and other dissenting sects were given the right to worship only in 1690, under the Toleration Act, but they had already established dozens of 'conventicles' in Sussex by then, in proud and open defiance of the authorities. In these times of inflamed religious passion, the vicar of Twineham's daughter married one of the 'Friends', and he set aside an area of his churchyard for them – so ensuring that his daughter should not have to be buried in unconsecrated ground.

A little problem remained, however. The Quakers loathed the tithing system, and they agreed to pay the vicar a modest annual rent for their plot only if he, in return, would give them a slightly larger sum for using the mown grass as animal fodder. The rector still pays his dues (four pence a year in new money) at a ceremony by the burial ground every third April.

BURIAL GROUND
Belonging to the
SOCIETY of FRIENDS
Quakers
marked by 4 corner stones
purchased in 1694
56 burials recorded
the last in 1732

The Quakers valued simplicity, and their burial ground at Twineham – unusually set within the Anglican churchyard – has no individual gravestones.

At the other extreme from such austere simplicity are the showy memorials so often favoured by the well-to-do. At Brightling the local squire and folly builder John 'Mad Jack' Fuller reinforced his reputation for eccentricity by having (in 1811, more than twenty years before his death) a monstrous pyramid constructed as his mausoleum.

Wildly extravagant in his architectural fancies, he was nonetheless utterly conventional in choosing lines from Gray's Elegy to appear on the wall:

The boast of heraldry, the pomp of power
And all that beauty, all that wealth
                                    e'er gave
Awaits alike th'inevitable hour,
The paths of glory lead but to the grave.

Nonconformist sects generally favour undemonstrative memorials, though the evangelist William Huntington (1745–1813) ordered himself a sizeable tomb with an arrogant epitaph 'dictated by himself' outside the Jireh Chapel in Lewes:

Here lies the coal-heaver who departed this life in the 69th year of his age, beloved of his God but abhorred of men. The Omniscient Judge at the Grand Assize shall ratify and confirm this to the confusion of many thousands, for England and its metropolis shall know that there hath been a prophet among them.

Many of our parish churchyards boast a few table tombs and the odd family vault, but the supreme 'valley of the dead' experience is a walk through the leafy 70 acres of the Lewes Road cemeteries at Brighton: 'hauntingly beautiful,' declares Maire McQueeney in her walker's guide; 'one of the most delightful spots in the whole of Brighton,' according to Antony Dale in his Brighton Cemeteries booklet.

'Mad Jack' Fuller's mausoleum in the churchyard at Brightling.

The earliest part (the then private Extra-Mural Cemetery, complete with catacombs and capacious family mausoleums), was laid out in 1850, anticipating an order which, on health grounds, prohibited any further burials in or around the town's churches and chapels. The parish burial ground (now Woodvale, and incorporating the borough crematorium) was opened next door to it a few years later: the local authority took over Woodvale in 1902 and the redundant Extra-Mural acres in 1956.

Here you will find the high and low of Victorian Brighton lying down together, a commendable democracy totally confounded by the pomp and circumstance affected by those with heavy pennies in their pockets. For here you can enjoy, albeit moss-covered and battered by the elements, a wide and wild variety of self-aggrandising memorials.

The most striking of them all *(back cover)* has a grieving pony on a huge white marble drum, with the hat, scarf and gloves of circus proprietor Fred Ginnett (died 1892) at its feet. The largest, its arrival demanding the demolition of a wall and the pulling power of twenty horses, is a Cornish granite sarcophagus ten feet tall by fifty feet wide to John Rastrick (died 1856), the engineer who built the London-to-Brighton railway line.

Fashions change, and recent years have seen a growing taste for photographs of the deceased on gravestones and for floral roadshine shrines to accident victims, but our modern way of death seems pallid when compared with this extravagance. For the ultimate in lavish and ornate memorials, however, we need to return to our country churchyard, enter the porch, lift the heavy latch and step inside.

The leafy Extra-Mural Cemetery at Brighton, designed by Amon Henry Wilds and dating from the 1850s. With neighbouring Woodvale it covers 70 acres off the Lewes Road and is a vivid testimony to the Victorian preoccupation with death.

AIN'T DEATH GRAND!

Only those at the very top of the social pile warranted a resting place inside the church in centuries past. Their riches, beyond the wildest imaginings of the peasantry, paid for sumptuous memorials in marble, painted alabaster and brass, occasionally in more humble wood and iron, and even, on occasion, in the local limestone which is known as Sussex, or Petworth, marble and comprises millions of compacted, fossilised snail shells.

Untouched by the weather, they have, of course, generally survived much better than their lowly counterparts outside, but the very standing of their occupants dictates that they are less likely to charm or amuse us with their quirkiness. Even a decent Tudor pun is botched for the sake of propriety: when Sir Nicholas Pelham died in 1559 the creator of his monument in St Michael's, Lewes, remembered that fourteen years earlier he had commanded troops which saw off a French raiding party:

WHAT TIME YE FRENCH SOUGHT TO
HAVE SACKT SEAFOORD
THIS PELHAM DID REPELL THEM BACK
ABOORD.

It should, without doubt, read *repell'em*, but either the engraver lost his nerve or someone tapped him on the shoulder.

The earliest memorials were slabs or coffin lids, often simply decorated with incised crosses, but large recumbent figures appear by the late thirteenth century and glowing monumental brasses by the early fourteenth.

There are good examples at every turn: Sussex, although its medieval churches are mostly small and not well represented in books of church architecture, has a reputation for the quality of its medieval and Tudor sepulchral monuments.

A few stand out for their beauty or their singularity. The earliest, dating from around 1145 (and now in St John's church, Southover, at Lewes), is the intricately carved tombstone in black Tournai marble to Gundrada, co-founder with her husband William de Warenne of Lewes Priory.

At Trotton the life-size figure of Margaret de Braose, Lady Camoys, is one of the earliest surviving brasses in England and the very first in honour of a woman: she died in 1310. Like the huge brass at Cowfold to Thomas Nelond, Prior of Lewes (died 1433), it was fashioned outside Sussex by brilliant metropolitan craftsmen.

This life-size early fourteenth century brass to Lady Camoys on the floor of the nave at Trotton is the oldest to be found anywhere in memory of a woman. Its Norman French inscription in Lombardic lettering translates: 'Margaret de Camoys lies here. God have mercy on her soul. Amen.'

At Amberley, John Wantele's brass of 1424 is the earliest known illustration of a tabard, while at Burton the brass to Lady Elizabeth Goring, who died in 1588, is the only example in the country of a woman wearing one. The representation of Sir Anthony St Leger (died 1539) at Slindon, although not similarly unique, is remarkable for being the only wooden effigy in the whole of Sussex. At Burwash a badly defaced early sixteenth century tomb slab in memory of John Collins is the earliest to have been made by the Wealden iron industry. At East Lavant Luci de Mildebi's tomb slab, made of Sussex marble, asks us (in Lombardic script similar to the Lady Camoys brass at Trotton) to pray for her soul – but who she was we don't know.

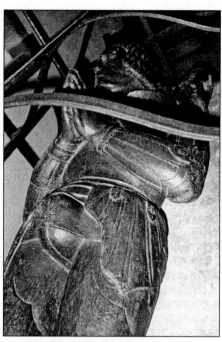

Proud codpiece and all. Sir Anthony St Leger's sixteenth century effigy at Slindon is the only wooden example in Sussex.

Other curiosities range from the small (heart burials can be seen at Chichester Cathedral and at Horsted Keynes) to the majestic: the chantry chapel built at Boxgrove in 1532 for Thomas de la Warr – an ornately carved creation, 'like a complete and improbable casket set down in one bay of the choir,' according to Ian Nairn – is a rare survivor of the Reformation's destructive iconoclasm. Masses would be said here for the souls of the

A detail from the De la Warr chantry at Boxgrove

dead man and his family. Nairn goes on to call it 'one of the very few really successful marriages of Gothic and Renaissance ornament anywhere in England.'

A few of our churches still carry reminders of long forgotten funeral practices. During the sixteenth and seventeenth centuries the deceased's armour (or a copy of it) was carried in the procession and later displayed in the church: Fletching and Racton still display these 'achievements'. And from early in the seventeenth century 'hatchments' (armorial tokens painted on board or canvas) accompanied the coffin, later to be hung on the dead man's house for several months before being deposited in the church.

More than a hundred of these can still be seen in Sussex, whereas there are no traces today of a third ceremonial feature, the virgins' wreaths which – a symbol of purity – were carried before the corpse of a young, unmarried woman and later hung in the church. How common this practice was is uncertain: Alfriston is the only Sussex church for which there is reliable evidence of it.

The grandest tombs, unsurprisingly, claimed the most prominent positions in the church – either close to the high altar in the chancel or near a subsidiary altar in the nave. Some even served as Easter Sepulchres and had the Sacrament displayed upon them during the Easter liturgy, a privilege specifically stipulated in the will of Thomas Fiennes, Lord Dacre, (who died in 1531) for his tomb at Herstmonceux.

To explore the county's tombs and wall monuments is to be made aware of changing fashions and, rather more profoundly, of changing sensibilities down the ages. An early fourteenth century tomb at Winchelsea shows an angel holding the dead man's soul in a napkin. During the fifteenth century the 'memento mori' theme is commonplace (a tomb at Arundel to the seventh Earl depicts a shrouded cadaver), but the medieval is gradually ousted by the Renaissance with its classical motifs. The typical Tudor tomb displays life-size recumbent effigies on table tombs with dutifully kneeling children beneath, but there is also a taste for more theatrical poses, with the deceased kneeling above his wife or sometimes (the tomb to Sir John Jefferay at Chiddingly) reclining on an elbow. 'The other effigies of this tomb,' writes Richard Marks, 'are shown as standing figures, a unique motif in English monuments of the pre-Civil War period. This grandiose *tableau vivant* exudes a self-confident and even secular air by no means untypical of Elizabethan and Jacobean tombs.'

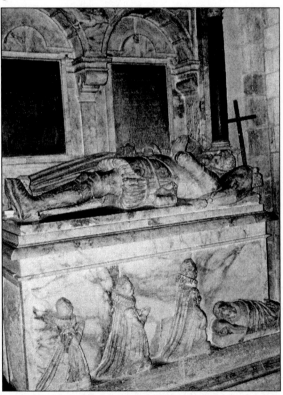

The alabaster tomb at Shipley to Sir Thomas Caryll (died 1616) and his wife is typical of the period, their recumbent figures lying side by side, while on the base their three kneeling daughters face their baby son in his cradle. The boy evidently died in infancy.

Four years, but a gulf of feeling, apart. John Ashburnham's tomb of 1671 *(below)* shows him dressed in armour between his two wives, with his children kneeling below. One of his wives is wearing a shroud: the symbolism of tombs instructs us that she died first.

William Ashburnham's monument of 1675 *(detail left)* depicts the dead man on his knees in a state of abject sorrow with his dying wife at his feet, crowned by a cherub.

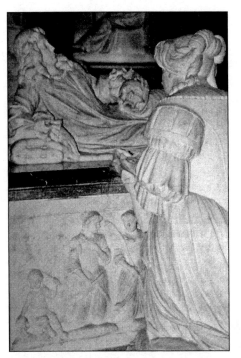

Enmarbled grief. The monument to Thomas Sackville at Withyham shows the thirteen-year-old boy with a skull in his hand, his heartbroken parents on either side.

William Ashburnham, hands held open in abject helplessness, above his wife Jane who, dying, is approached by a winged cherub bearing a crown.

At Withyham *(left)* a chapel was built to house the amazing marble monument to Thomas Sackville, who died in 1677 at the age of thirteen. The boy, reclining, holds a skull in his hand, while his parents, the fifth Earl and Countess of Dorset, kneel to either side of him: 'A directness of feeling and expression,' declares Nikolaus Pevsner, 'unprecedented in England.'

These outbursts of feeling later give way to a more sober classical style, with the inclusion of allegorical figures. At Cuckfield, the figure of Truth holds a mirror in one hand and a portrait medallion of Charles Sergison (died 1732) in the other.

And then comes palpable sorrow. The two outstanding monuments of the seventeenth century – both using life-size figures to express inconsolable grief – are to be found in the east of the county, at Ashburnham and at Withyham. The change in feeling, or at least in the expression of it, is especially marked at Ashburnham, where two very different tombs *(facing page)* stand practically side by side.

John Ashburnham's, fashioned in 1671, is strictly traditional: he lies, dressed in armour, between his two wives (one seen in her shroud) with the obligatory children kneeling below. The other, designed only four years later, depicts a distraught

Classical allegory at Cuckfield: Truth looking in a mirror and holding a portrait medallion of Charles Sergison.

17

Sentimentality begins to take hold during the eighteenth century, a period of draped urns, child angels and weeping women in flowing robes, although there is nothing spurious in the carved relief of 1752 at Boxgrove *(right)* which shows the Countess of Derby sitting under a tree and offering comfort to the poor of the parish: she had in life endowed almshouses and a school.

A friend to the poor. A sarcophagus at Boxgrove shows Mary, Countess of Derby (died 1752), succouring the needy.

Later generations were encouraged to extend this charity to the church fabric (organs, stained glass windows and the like) rather than spend vast amounts on their tombs, with the result that both the size and the quality of memorials declined – although this did not, of course, prevent the pompous from parading their virtues in fancy epitaphs on the church walls.

The finest reply to this funereal swank is to be found on an old gravestone now propped in the church porch at Poling. We know nothing about Alice Woolldridge other than that she was Robert's wife and died in 1740, but her epitaph is eloquent.

The words, incidentally, are found in other parts of the country, and the mason has to make a choice at the end of the fourth line between correct grammar and the satisfaction of the rhyme: our man, I think, made the right decision:

> *The World is a round thing*
> *And full of crooked streets,*
> *Death is a market place*
> *Where all men meets.*
> *If Life was a thing*
> *That money could buy*
> *The Rich would live*
> *And the poor would dye.*

Alice Woolldridge's 'World is a round thing' gravestone at Poling.

WORDS TO THE WISE

Reader by whatsoever motive led
To view these gloomy mansions of the dead
Remember life's a transient breath,
Therefore prepare 'gainst sudden death
Begin therefore, prepare today,
Lest you like me are snatch'd away.

It's difficult to know what arouses our greater sympathy for John Packham, who lies in the churchyard at Cuckfield: his sudden death at 51 (not a bad innings in 1787) or the blatant manipulation of his misfortune by someone who couldn't resist drawing a moral from it.

The awfulness of death can make philosophers of the dullest among us, (those seventeenth century skulls and crossbones are themselves a mute but terrible reminder of what awaits us all), yet it seems a bit much if nothing better can be said of a man's life but that its ending should somehow improve the rest of us.

The parishioners at Worth perhaps remembered for a generation who Mr T.S. was, but his gravestone carries only his initials and a sententious message:

> MY FRIENDS SO
> DEAR AS YOU PAS
> BY SOE AS YOU ARE
> SOE ONCE WAS I
> AND AS I AM
> SOE SHALL YOU BE
> REMEMBER
> DEATH AND
> THINK ON ME.

These lines, with variants, are common in the seventeenth and early eighteenth centuries. There are examples at Singleton (John Nye, died 1748) and neighbouring West Dean (Mary Mitchell, 1724).

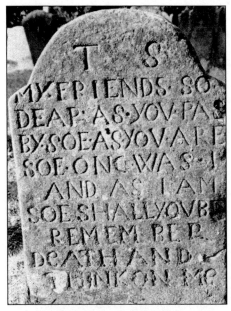

'Remember Death and think on me' – a common theme on our older gravestones. This one at Worth remembers the dead man only by his initials.

A chilling verse could once be seen outside Chichester Cathedral:

> *Thou wandering ghost*
> *Take home this rhyme,*
> *Next grave that opens*
> *May be thine.*

Untimely deaths are obviously more likely to provoke deep thoughts and dire warnings, particularly when the victims are young children. Twelve-year-old George Tulley, an only child, was accidentally shot on January 6, 1882, and is buried at Lower Beeding:

> *A sudden change, he in a moment fell*
> *and had not time to bid farewell.*
> *Think nothing strange, death*
> *happens to us all*
> *Our lot Today, Tomorrow thine may fall.*

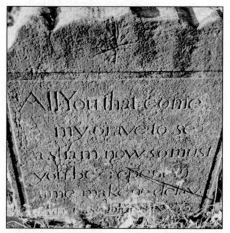

'All You that come my grave to see/as I am now so must you be'. This typical moralising gravestone at Hartfield urges us to 'repent in time, make no delay'.

Ann Varnham's tomb at Lindfield is another which urges us to do the right thing before it's too late. She died in 1840 at the age of 24:

Pray, young people, when this you see
Prepare your lives to follow me.
My time was short, my glass was run
God thought it best to call me home.

What the right thing might be few epitaphs are bothered to tell us, but William Coppard's stone of 1804 at Cuckfield manages (in one of the worst verses to be found in a Sussex churchyard) to spell matters out:

Frail mortal men be holy, good & wise
Be on your guard and serve the Lord always
for death will come how soon we know not
             when
be well prepared to meet your Christian
             heaven.

A similar message appears on the stone at West Hoathly to Jane Comber, who died in 1805:

All who pass his way along
think how sudden was she gone
God does not always them forgive
Therefore be careful how you live.

Another, at Hartfield (on the footstone of Thomas Young, *p. 8*), reveals a mason with no idea of rhymed endings to lines:

Death is the painful
way that all Must
Tread. Joyful for
them who are by
Virtue Led.

Few have trowelled on the moral more thickly than the versifier of the Nailard tomb at Bolney. If he was John Nailard himself he deserves our pity, since he lost his twenty-six-year-old wife Mary and his young sons William and Thomas within the space of a few months in 1777:

Young men and women all attend
and often view your latter end
begin and end in virtues ways
in this employment spend your days
more joy by such a course you'll find
than can be thought by human mind
death find me in gloom of years
I hope for bliss when Christ appears
Surrounded with heavenly train
to give His servants endless gain.

It's assumed that the epitaph inside Hartfield church to the former rector Richard Randes (died 1640) was his own composition. If it wasn't, then his flock evidently held him in low esteem. It reads, in a translation from the Latin:

He lived obscure and always shunned the
vulgar throng, that is wont to reek
of the odours of vine-crowned Bacchus. But
alas! he lived badly and now
imprisoned in the darkness of the tomb, he
teacheth thee what he late began
to learn himself.

The dread of having someone else make bricks from our spent straw, as it were, should perhaps encourage us to devise our own epitaphs in good time. John Olliver, the eccentric miller whose tomb sits alone on the Downs above Worthing, planned himself a colourful send-off, with the mourners dressed in bright clothing and a young girl to read the burial service.

At one end of his tomb, bas-relief figures of Time and Death appear above a sonnet (thought to have been written by Olliver himself), whose literary standard is well above the monumental average:

Death, why so fast? pray stop your hand
And let my glass run out its sand:
As neither Death nor Time will stay,
Let us improve the present day.
Why start you at that skeleton?
'Tis your own picture which you shun.
Alive it did resemble thee
And thou when dead like that shall be:
But tho' Death must have his will,
Yet old Time prolongs the date,
Till the measure we shall fill
That's allotted us by Fate.
When that's done, then TIME and DEATH
Both agree to take our breath!

The miller's tomb at Highdown, above Worthing. John Olliver thought long about his own death.

John Fuller's memorial in the chancel at Uckfield (a large iron slab with brass inlays) likewise pays Death his dues. Fuller died on April 6, 1610, but how old he was we don't know: someone forgot to fill in the gap on his brass which had carefully been left to record it. His epitaph ends with a sombre quatrain:

Now I am dead and layd in grounde
And that my bones are rotten
By this shall I remembred be
Or else I am forgotten.

Something even more gruesome can be seen at Poling, in the concluding lines of the epitaph to Henry Jackson (died 1773) and his wife Mary:

Although we lie confind with worms and dust
We hope in Christ to rise among the just

Stern finger-wagging on the stone of William Harris at Bexhill *(page 31)* is directed specifically at those of us who enjoy churchyard visiting:

OH! LET MY SUDDEN DOOM
A WARNING BE TO ALL.
EEN WHILE THOU BENDEST O'ER MY TOMB
THOU MAYST AS QUICKLY FALL

And yet, although most tombstone reflections upon the sad fact of our mortality dwell, understandably, upon the darker side of things, a cheerful few do their bit to lift the moral weight from our poor shoulders.

John Harland (who died in 1764 and is buried at Steyning) offers us a merry quip from beyond the grave:

Life's a jest, all things
show it
I thought so once and
now I know it.

21

Two headstones at Walberton which show fatal accidents in remarkable detail.

Young Ann Rusbridger *(left)* was killed when a barrel fell from a passing cart and struck her.

Charles Cook *(below)* met his end under a felled tree, and we see the woodman holding up his hand in horror at what he has done. Death wields an arrow, Time holds an hour-glass and a scythe, the angels blow their trumpets and God sits in glory with his Book of Judgement at the ready.

OUT OF THE BLUE

Shot, drowned and run over; burned, suffocated, mangled by machinery: to study Sussex gravestones is to be reminded of how many ways death may catch us unawares. This chapter of accidents and other abrupt ends is regrettably only a selection of such horrors, focusing on the more striking and sometimes surprisingly detailed epitaphs we can find scattered about our churchyards.

Crushed by a tree

None is more vivid than the stone at Walberton to Charles Cook. The inscription informs us that he 'lost His Life by the fall of a tree' in 1767, but the marvellously graphic scene above it *(facing page)* tells us rather more. Poor Charles lies beneath the tree, his tricorn hat behind him, while a woodman – with an axe in his hand and another tool positioned beneath the roots – acknowledges his sorry role in the affair. Here we have, too, a wide range of motifs typical of the period: Time with scythe and hour-glass; Death wielding an arrow; Scales of Justice; trumpeting angels; and God sitting in glory with his Book of Judgement. An undoubted masterpiece.

Struck by a barrel

The headstone to eight-year-old Ann Rusbridger *(facing page)* in the same churchyard is far less finely carved, but equally specific. She was struck by a falling barrel and, again, the unwitting agent of her death (the local carter?) holds up his hands in shock. The date was September 25, 1802, and a short verse rehearses the 'memento mori' theme:

> With my companions at our childish play
> God sent the blow that took my life away
> My death was sudden by the Lord's decree
> I am gone first and you will follow me.

For teasing a mule

The phrase 'childish play' crops up again on a far plainer gravestone close to the entrance of All Saints Church in Hastings: like 'hopes in Heaven to meet again' it seems to have been one of the stock phrases available to masons and their versifiers, but has it ever been the prelude to such a terrible story as this? John Archdeacon was nine years old when he died on June 5, 1820:

> Here lies an only darling boy
> Who was his widow'd mother's joy,
> Her grief and sad affliction prove
> How tenderly she did him love.
>
> In childish play he teased a mule
> Which rag'd its owner's angry soul
> And thro' whose cruel blows and spleen
> This child so soon a corpse was seen.
>
> This Mother now is left to mourn
> The loss of her beloved Son
> Tho' sighs and tears will prove in vain
> She hopes in Heaven to meet again.

The owner of the mule, William Picknell, was charged at Lewes Assizes with 'feloniously killing and slaying' the boy, but he was acquitted.

A blighted village

Inside the churchyard gate at Kirdford is a memorial remarkable for the terrible story it tells. For here, within the space of only a few months, three separate accidents took the lives of no fewer than seven villagers. We can well imagine the mason shuddering as he steadily added one name after another to the stone:

TO THE MEMORY OF
GEORGE NEWMAN AGED 17
CHARLES NEWMAN AGED 13
THOMAS RAPLEY AGED 14
GEORGE PUTTICK AGED 13
AND WILLIAM BOXALL AGED 19 YEARS,
WHO DIED AT SLADELAND ON THE 21ST
JANUARY 1838
FROM HAVING PLACED GREEN WOOD
ASHES IN THEIR BEDROOM

IN THE MIDST OF LIFE WE ARE IN DEATH

EDWARD EVERSHED WHO DIED ON THE
25TH JAN. 1838
FROM A FALL FROM A HORSE, AGED 37
YEARS

ALSO

THOMAS EAMES, AGED 14 YEARS, WHO
DIED ON THE 26TH MARCH 1838 FROM A
FARMERS CART PASSING OVER HIM.

The stone recording Kirdford's darkest year.

The five lads who suffocated together, houseboys at Sladelands, had taken a bucket of hot ashes from under the bread oven to warm their bedroom, not knowing that a broken window (the only means of ventilation) had been repaired.

Accidentally shot

Death by firearm is a fate widely recorded on Sussex gravestones. A very young victim is buried at Thakeham:

In loving memory of William Alfred
beloved grandson of the above
& only son of William and Jessie Cripps who
was accidentally shot July 1st 1910 aged 7
years.

At St Matthew's church, Silverhill in St Leonards, the steps to the lectern are a memorial to 18-year-old Richard Gould, 'accidentally shot abroad' in 1906.

Dying away from home was also the fate of Joseph Gamble, whose grave is at Walberton:

Here lieth the body of
Joseph Papforth Gamble
(Late of FOUNTAIN ABBEY
PRADE STREET, LONDON)
who lost his life by an
Accident when shooting
on the 20th of January
1841
In the 65th Year of his Age.

At Worth (where, on an explosive theme, we should note that Robert Whitehead, inventor of the first successful torpedo, is buried) we find a female victim:

M.S. Elizabeth Clifton wife of Henry Clifton
who died at The Grove in this parish by the
accidental explosion of a gun 11 Sept 1826
aged 35 years.

'Unfortunately shot.' Smugglers like Daniel Skayles were not regarded as criminals by the community at large.

Smugglers

It was rarely an accident when a smuggler was shot, and just as rare for his epitaph to acknowledge his guilt. Thirty-one-year-old William Cowerson was killed by an excise officer on a moonlit night in February, 1832, during the last major smuggling affray in Sussex, but the church bells are said to have rung 'a merry peal' nevertheless when he was buried at Steyning:

Death with his dart did pierce my heart
When I was in my prime
Grieve not for me my dearest friends
For it was God's appointed time.
Our life hangs by a single thread
Which soon is cut and we are dead
Therefore repent make no delay
For in my bloom I was call'd away.

Daniel Skayles was also caught, and killed, in the act, but his gravestone at Patcham records only regret, an improving message – and a strangely precise time of death:

Sacred to the memory of
DANIEL SKAYLES Aged 34 Years
who was unfortunately Shot
on Thursday Evening
Nov. 17 1796

Alas! swift flew the fatal lead,
Which piercèd through the young man's
head
He instant fell, resigned his breath,
And closed his languid eyes in death.
All you who do this stone draw near,
Oh! pray let fall the pitying tear.
From this sad instance may we all
Prepare to meet Jehovah's call.

All of our surviving smugglers' stones are sadly weather-worn, none more so than the one in All Saints churchyard, Hastings, which tells the sorry tale of Joseph Swain – whose career as a 'free-trader' has to be registered as unproven:

This Stone
Sacred to the memory of
JOSEPH SWAIN, Fisherman
was created at the expence of
the members of the friendly
Society of Hastings
in commiseration of his cruel and untimely
death and as a record of the public indignation
at the needless and sanguinary violence of
which he was the unoffending Victim. He
was shot by Geo. England, one of the
Sailors employ'd in the Coast blockade
service in open day on the 13th March 1821
and almost instantly expir'd, in the twenty-
ninth year of his age, leaving a Widow and
five small children to lament his loss.

England, who had attempted to search Swain's boat, was found guilty of murder but was later pardoned – to the fury of the Hastings fishermen.

Acts of God

If winning the lottery is statistically a more likely bet than being struck by lightning, a bolt from the blue that takes two friends together is, with due respect to the Almighty, one of the cruellest Acts of God imaginable. So it was on a summer's day in 1907, as their gravestone at Goring tells us:

Memorial of a sort: this pub sign at Lewes portrays Britain's worst ever avalanche. The victims are buried at South Malling.

SIDNEY CHARLES   FREDERICK BENNETT
ORCHARD   WADY
AGED 19   AGED 22
WHO WERE KILLED BY LIGHTNING NEAR
HIGHDOWN COTTAGES ON SUNDAY
JUNE 9th 1907.
IN THEIR DEATH THEY WERE NOT DIVIDED.

The young men, who died instantly, had taken shelter under an elm with two fellow farm workers, Arthur Winton and Wady's father, James.

It may well have been lightning that killed the local butcher Henry Weller, his wife Mary and Elizabeth Bincham one dreadful night outside Lewes but, as we learn from their headstone at Glynde (now propped with others against the churchyard wall), their bodies lay undiscovered for hours. The three

MET THEIR DEATH ON THE HIGH
ROAD NEAR RANSCOMBE
DURING AN AWFUL THUNDER STORM
ON THE NIGHT OF JUNE 24 1863
THE CART IN WHICH THEY HAD
TRAVELLED WAS OVERTHROWN AND
NEAR IT THEY WERE FOUND LYING
DEAD EARLY IN THE MORNING OF JUNE
25TH.

Death by lightning may be rare, but to be smothered by an avalanche in Sussex of all places is surely the worst luck imaginable. A plaque at South Malling,

Lewes, remembers the victims of the worst such disaster Britain has known:

THIS TABLET
IS PLACED HERE BY SUBSCRIPTION
TO RECORD AN AWFUL INSTANCE
OF THE
UNCERTAINTY OF HUMAN LIFE
ON THE MORNING OF THE 27th DEC
1836

THE POOR HOUSE OF THIS PARISH
WAS DESTROYED BY A MASS OF SNOW
FALLING FROM THE HILL ABOVE, AND
THE
FOLLOWING EIGHT INDIVIDUALS WERE
BURIED BENEATH THE RUINS.

The names follow, their ages ranging from 82 to fifteen. The Snowdrop Inn, by the Cuilfail tunnel, marks the spot of the disaster today.

From his memorial at Rye, we learn that a particularly nasty end awaited William Barham:

who, whilst attempting to ride in the night through the haven of this town to the farther side, a storm having suddenly arisen, was overwhelmed in the slime and waves, and unfortunately perished on April 2nd, 1717, aged 36.

As they would like to have gone

A heart attack while in full throat is the fate which befell William Kensett:

> who fell asleep in Jesus while
> singing the following lines
> in Divine Service in Bolney Chapel
> September 8th 1889
> "Of all the joys we mortals know
> Jesus thy love exceeds the rest,
> Love the best blessing here below
> the nearest image of the Blest.
> While we are held in thy embrace
> there's not a thought attempts to rove,
> Each smile upon Thy Beauteous Face
> Fixes and charms and fires our love."

Quite how far William managed to get through these lines we aren't told.

Michael Turner, clerk and sexton at Warnham for fifty years, was another man who went as he presumably would have

Michael Turner's headstone at Warnham. He died playing his fiddle.

wished – in his case while playing his beloved violin. His church's leading musician, he was also a colourful character, who dressed in a white smock frock and, for Sunday best, an old-fashioned beaver high hat. Whoever wrote his epitaph knew how to turn a rhyme:

> HIS DUTY DONE, BENEATH THIS STONE
> OLD MICHAEL LIES AT REST.
> HIS RUSTIC RIG, HIS SONG, HIS JIG
> WERE EVER OF THE BEST.
>
> WITH NODDING HEAD THE CHOIR HE LED
> THAT NONE SHOULD START TOO SOON.
> THE SECOND, TOO, HE SANG FULL TRUE,
> HIS VIOL PLAYED THE TUNE.
>
> AND WHEN AT LAST HIS AGE HAD PASSED
> ONE HUNDRED LESS ELEVEN
> WITH FAITHFUL CLING TO FIDDLE STRING
> HE SANG HIMSELF TO HEAVEN.

Murder!

Edward Alldredge's epitaph at All Saints Church, Hastings, reports that he was 'maliciously shot' on April 26, 1806. leaving us to guess at the details, but the occasional headstone is more specific in registering a death as unequivocal murder.

In the old Jewish cemetery in Hollingdean Road, Brighton, is the grave of the borough's first chief constable, Henry Solomon

> WHO WAS BRUTALLY MURDERED
> WHILE IN THE PUBLIC DISCHARGE
> OF THE DUTIES OF HIS OFFICE
> ON THE 14TH DAY OF MARCH 1844
> IN THE FIFTIETH YEAR OF HIS AGE.

Solomon was attacked with a poker by John Lawrence, whose execution the following April 6 was the last public hanging at Horsham.

A grim tale of butchery is told on a graveslab set into the church floor at Rye:

Here lyeth the body of ALLEN GREBELL, ESQ, who, having served the office of Mayor of this town for ten years with the greatest honour and integrity, fell by the cruel stab of a sanguinary butcher, on March 17th 1742.

The butcher was a vengeful man named Breeds, who had intended to kill Grebell's brother-in-law, Thomas Lamb, but mistook his victim on a dark night. After his execution the following year, his body was left to rot in a cage out on the marshes.

'Washed Ashore'. Grave of an unknown sailor at Friston.

Death by water

Drowning is an all too common fate in a coastal county, as many of our graveyards bear witness. Sometimes the bodies are never identified: a cross at Friston with the simple epitaph 'Washed Ashore' is moving in its terrible anonymity, while a similarly poignant memorial at neighbouring East Dean carries the words 'Known unto God'.

We are better informed about the fate of Thomas Barrow, master of the sloop *Two Brothers*, since his headstone at Bosham both describes his end and *(facing page)* illustrates it. A horse, in a definition of 1711, was 'a conveniency for the Men to tread on, in going out to furl the Sails':

*In Memory of
THOMAS Son of Richard and Ann
BARROW Master of the Sloop Two
Brothers who by the Breaking of the
Horse fell into the Sea & was Drown'd
October the 13th 1759 Aged 23 Years*

*Though Boreas's storms and Neptune's
            waves
    have tos'd me to and fro
Yet I at length by Gods decree
    am harbour'd here below
Where at an Anchor here I lay
    with many of our Fleet
Yet once again I shall set Sail
    my Saviour Christ to meet.*

Many a fisherman has been lost off our coast and many, like George Ragless at South Bersted, were taken in the prime of life. Six months earlier the local paper had reported his wedding, with fishermen's gear hoisted on poles and 'a demand for bunting all the day and for fiddle strings all the night'. The verse on his headstone has an unusual lilt:

*Sacred to the Memory of GEORGE RAGLESS
who was drowned off Bognor in a storm
May 23 1867 Aged 21 Years.*

*Brought up from his youth on the billow
He sailed o'er the fathomless deep
And now the cold earth is his pillow
And sound and unbroken his sleep.
Here no winds and no waves overtake him
No tempests can ever arise
But the voice of the Saviour shall wake him
And bid him ascend to the skies.*

Thomas Barrow's headstone at Boshom shows him falling from his sloop.

A memorial complete with vivid disaster scene in the Central Bandstand on Eastbourne seafront remembers John Wesley Woodward:

The Titanic sinks on an Eastbourne memorial.

WHO, WITH OTHERS OF THE HERO-MUSICIANS OF THE SHIP'S BAND, PERISHED IN THE ATLANTIC THROUGH THE SINKING OF THE WHITE STAR LINER TITANIC ON APRIL 15TH 1912.

Another shipwreck is commemorated at Newhaven, where an impressive monument records the sinking of *HMS Brazen* on January 26, 1800, with the loss of more than a hundred lives. The captain was James Hanson, and his epitaph notes a cruel irony:

It was the will of heaven to preserve him during four years voyage of danger and difficulty round the world on discoveries with Captn Vancouver in the years 1791 1792 1793 1794 but to take him from us when most he thought himself secure.

At Rye Harbour stands a memorial to the seventeen men (many of them related) who drowned when their lifeboat, the *Mary Stanford*, capsized in a storm in the early hours of November 15, 1928. There are other tributes to the men in the churches at Rye (a tablet of Manx stone) and at Winchelsea, where a stained glass window by Douglas Strachan is inscribed with words written by Sir Henry Newbolt:

In the darkness of their supreme hour they stayed not to weigh doubt or danger but freely offering their portion in this life for the ransom of men whom they had never known they went boldly into the last of all their storms.

Grief of a private kind is expressed at Ewhurst Green, where five-year-old William Jacobson drowned in a pond in his father's garden at Lordine Farm on March 16, 1905. A stained glass window shows the youngster sitting on Christ's knee above a Biblical text: 'My thoughts are not your thoughts, neither are your ways my ways saith the Lord.'

Robert White of the 11th Regiment of Light Dragoons met his death at Glyne Gap on March 6, 1804, while exercising his horse on the sands. He must have been thrown into the sea, for his epitaph at Bexhill reads:

On Duty Cheerful and in Battle Brave,
Yet Fell a Victim to the foaming Wave.

Death by natives

The white man's burden in our glorious days of empire included the risk of being attacked by natives who failed to realise the good we were doing them – sometimes with fatal results.

Henry Lushington, who has a large memorial complete with bust in St Mary's church in Eastbourne Old Town, survived the notorious Black Hole of Calcutta only to be killed seven years later aged 26:

In ye Year 1756, by a melancholy Revolution, He was with Others to ye Amount of 146 forced into a Dungeon at CALCUTTA so small that 23 only escaped Suffocation. He was one of ye Survivors, but reserved for greater Misery, for by a Subsequent Revolution in the Year 1763 He was with 200 more taken Prisoners at PATNA, and after a tedious Confinement being singled out with JOHN ELLIS and WILLIAM HAY Esq. was by the Order of the Nabob COSSIM ALLY KAWN and under ye Direction of One SOMEROO, an Apostate European, deliberately and inhumanly murdered.

Hay, who died with him, came from Glynde.

At Stopham there's a memorial to 29-year-old Major Edmund Musgrave Barttelot, killed while on an expedition to the Congo with Henry Morton Stanley who, seventeen years earlier, had found Dr David Livingstone in the African jungle. The party had split up:

MAJOR BARTTELOT LEFT ENGLAND IN 1887, AND WHILE IN CHARGE OF A LARGE EXPEDITION IN SEARCH OF STANLEY, AND FOR THE RELIEF OF EMIN PASHA, WAS TREACHEROUSLY SHOT AT UNARIA IN CENTRAL AFRICA 19TH JULY 1888, BY SENGA, A NATIVE MANYEMA CARRIER, PROVIDED BY TIPPOO TIB.

Bishop James Hannington, son of the man who founded the Brighton store, has a memorial in St George's church at Hurstpierpoint, where he served as curate-in-charge for nearly nine years. He resigned to join the Church Missionary Society and in 1884 was consecrated first Bishop in East Equatorial Africa:

HE LEFT ENGLAND AGAIN THE SAME YEAR AND STARTED FROM FRERE TOWN IN THE FOLLOWING JULY TO OPEN UP A NEW ROUTE TO HIS MOST DISTANT STATION IN UGANDA, AND ON REACHING THE NORTH EAST SHORE OF THE VICTORIA NYANZA WAS EXECUTED BY ORDER OF MWANGA THE KING, ON THE 29TH OCTOBER 1885.

Riding for a fall

A six-sided hollow stone tower near Pulborough known as the Toat Monument has a plaque above its doorway inscribed 'In memory of Samuel Drinkald, 1823'.

Drinkald, a London tea merchant, was killed here when he fell from his horse.

The Toat Monument marks the spot where Samuel Drinkald took a fatal fall.

At Withyham, a monument of 1815 to George John Frederick, 4th Duke of Dorset, tells us that he died in Dublin after falling from his horse.

Young Job Guy, who is buried at Chalvington, was killed by a horse, but without getting up on its back. He 'departed this life by a kick from a horse 17th April 1878, aged 8 years and 2 weeks.'

Death on the road

Car and motorcycle accidents feature on a sprinkling of gravestones, but fatalities were more unusual on our roads in the days of horse-drawn transport. A plaque on the wall at Portslade gives us some painful detail:

> In Memory of JOHN the affectionate son of JOHN and MARY ANNE BORRER who by an awful dispensation of Providence on the 10th day after his marriage was suddenly cut off and separated from his beloved wife and all who are dear to him by a coach accident on entering the city of Carlisle on 17th August 1844 aged 29 years. Having endured with remarkable fortitude the amputation of his leg, he died after 3 days of acute suffering leaving his family in deep affliction.

In the churchyard at Battle is a table tomb to Robert Compton:

> A COMMERCIAL TRAVELLER
> WHO WAS KILLED NEAR THIS SPOT
> BY BEING THROWN FROM HIS GIG
> ON THE 28TH OF MAY 1839,
> IN THE 29TH YEAR OF HIS AGE

while at Bexhill we find a stone to William Harris:

> WHO WAS ACCIDENTALLY KILLED IN THE
> PARISH OF ST MARYS BULVERHYTHE
> BY HIS WAGGON PASSING OVER HIM
> ON THE 27TH OF JANUARY 1869

Beside the road from Partridge Green to West Grinstead, close to the railway bridge, is a monument to W.H.W.R. Burrell, second son of Sir W.W. Burrell Bt:

> WHO THROUGH AN
> ACCIDENT THAT BEFELL
> HIM AT THIS SPOT WAS
> SUDDENLY CALLED TO THE
> PRESENCE OF HIS CREATOR
> 19 JULY 1883 AGED 26 YEARS

He was killed in a fall from his bicycle.

Death on the line

Railway accidents are mentioned on several memorials, but one of them has a special place in the record books: William Huskisson, the MP for Chichester, was the first man to be killed by a railway engine.

His memorial in the Cathedral tells us that his death 'changed a scene of triumphant rejoicing into one of general mourning,' adding that 'he relinquished this position when yielding to a sense of publick duty'. In reality he misjudged the speed of Stephenson's *Rocket* when crossing the line to talk to the Duke of Wellington at the opening of the Liverpool and Manchester Railway. Stephenson took Huskisson fifteen miles to hospital on an engine, but he died the same night.

Huskisson lived at Eartham, and his wife raised another memorial in the parish church. The wording is similar. He died on September 15, 1830:

> HAVING BORNE WITH CHRISTIAN
> FORTITUDE AND RESIGNATION THE
> DREADFUL SUFFERANCE WHICH
> CLOSED HIS LIFE AND CONVERTED A
> DAY OF REJOICING INTO ONE OF
> NATIONAL CALAMITY.

Occupational hazards

Death at the workplace is recorded on several gravestones in Sussex, but few are as specific as the epitaph to a young butcher who worked a literal stone's throw from his last resting place just inside the churchyard wall at Chailey:

SACRED
TO THE MEMORY
OF
THOMAS JEFFERY
WHO DIED 18TH OCTOBER 1852
AGED 18 YEARS

WHEN PURSUING HIS TRADE AS A BUTCHER
HIS KNIFE SLIPPED AND
SEVERED THE MAIN ARTERY OF HIS THIGH
AFTER WHICH HE LIVED ONLY ONE HOUR.
THUS SUDDENLY IN GOD'S PROVIDENCE
WAS THIS YOUNG COMMUNICANT TAKEN
TO HIS REST.

An unlucky butcher whose knife slipped: Thomas Jeffery's headstone at Chailey.

Mill machinery was a constant hazard. The headstone of a victim at Hamsey reminds us not only of the grief but of the potential ruin the death of a breadwinner could leave behind. William Walker was caught in the mill machinery and 'killed in an instant' on February 9, 1832. He was 44 years of age:

BY ACCIDENT FROM LABOUR TORN
A FATHER SLEEPS BELOW.
TWELVE CHILDREN AND THEIR MOTHER
MOURN
THE KEENNESS OF THE BLOW.
THAT HIS SAD FATE MAY MAY LONG BE
KNOWN
AND LONG RECORDED HERE
HIS ELDER SONS ERECT THIS STONE
AND ASK THE READER'S TEAR.

At Uckfield the gravestone of 47-year-old John Baker, buried here in 1872, states simply that he was:

killed by machinery.

Baker, captain of the local Bonfire Boys, ran an engine which drove machinery at a local joinery. On the day of his death he had started work early, and his workmates found his body by the machine when they arrived – his clothing caught in the drive shaft and his head smashed.

Windmills had a bad safety record, what with fire, moving machinery and the revolving sweeps, and not only the workers were at risk. A headstone in South Bersted churchyard tells how a little girl was killed at her father's mill – Old Broyle Mill, near Chichester:

*In Memory of Louisa
daughter of Edmund and Mary Peachey
who was unfortunately killed
by the sweep of a windmill,
May 25th, 1827, in the 4th year of her age.*

Diseases

So many people were taken by disease in days gone by that it's rather surprising to find so few references to it. Perhaps the very familiarity stayed the mason's hand.

At West Tarring the cause of death *is* spelt out on the tomb of John Parson, with dialect for 'fourth' – 'buryed the fowerth day of March 1683':

> YOUTH WAS HIS AGE
> VIRGINITY HIS STATE
> LEARNING HIS LOVE
> CONSUMPTION HIS FATE.

Travelling abroad brought obvious health risks, as memorials to two cholera victims remind us. On the chancel wall at Hartfield is a plaque to H.S. Polehampton, chaplain to the East India Company, who died of the disease in 1857 during the siege of Lucknow, after being wounded.

The other, inside the church at Warnham, speaks quietly of parental loss:

> IN LOVING MEMORY OF
> FREDERICK MURRAY LUCAS
> YOUNGEST SON OF C.T. LUCAS
> OF WARNHAM COURT.
> WHO DIED SUDDENLY FROM CHOLERA
> AT SURAT. INDIA
> WHILE TRAVELLING ROUND THE WORLD
> BORN 3 FEB^Y 1860 DIED 7 NOV^R 1887.

And then smallpox – and a reminder at Northiam that the intended cure was sometimes itself fatal:

> *Michael, son of Michael and Mary Woolett of Playden in this county, died in this psh of inoculation against smallpox, 4th April 1764.*

It was in 1775 that Edward Jenner made the study of cowpox which was to lead to the smallpox inoculations still in use today (as we've seen, there had been earlier, less successful attempts), so it's something

'Consumption his fate': John Parson's tomb at West Tarring.

of a coincidence that 38-year-old Phillip Jenner should have died 'of the smallpox' in Cuckfield on April 25 in that very same year. The opportunistic writer of his epitaph treated the headstone as a kind of advertising hoarding. Let's hope his efforts were successful:

> *Kind reader stop & drop a tear*
> *for him who now lies sleeping here*
> *a husband, loving parent kind*
> *a friend and neighbour good you'll find*
> *his widow left in great distress*
> *with six small children fatherless*
> *but may God of his goodness send*
> *to them a kind assisting friend.*

Two years later a victim was buried at St Anne's churchyard, Lewes:

> IN MEMORY OF
> JOHN STONE who died
> of the Small Pox
> Feb. 27 1777 Aged
> 42 Years.

In the tower of the church at Cocking is the gravestone of Sarah White, who died at the age of 25 in 1772:

> *Weep not for me my parents dear,*
> *Since God was pleased to lay me here.*
> *It was the smallpox I did crave*
> *Which now has brought me to my grave.*

The word 'crave' here means 'fear' (as in craven), rather than 'desire'.

Even a death as unpleasant as this could prompt a play on the victim's ugly rash, as we find on an old tomb outside Chichester Cathedral:

Here Lyeth the Body of
MARY the Wife of M^R EDW^D
CRAMBORNE who through ye
spotted Veil of ye Small Pox
rendered a pure and unspotted
Soul to God expecting
but never fearing Death
which ended her Days
May the 9: 1722
AGED 38 YEARS

Flying accidents

Not only does the churchyard at Tangmere have numerous headstones to English and German pilots killed during the last war (see p. 51), but here you will also find the graves of several pilots killed in accidents – sometimes during flying displays. Let one suffice for them all:

SERGT PILOT
JEFFERY JOHN TANFIELD
(DEAR BILLY)
KILLED IN FLYING ACCIDENT
EMPIRE DAY 1937
AGED 20 YEARS.

Death by burning

In Broadwater cemetery we find Minnie Tellick's parents attempting to come to terms with their grief:

DIED FROM ACCIDENTAL BURNING
APRIL 26TH 1873
IN THE 18TH YEAR OF HER AGE

Her sorrowing parents erect this humble Memorial to a child beloved and deeply lamented, but their sorrow is tempered and consoled by hope.

"For of such is the Kingdom of Heaven."

MANY A SLIP

'I went to Bolney,' wrote Thomas Marchant of Hurstpierpoint in his diary on July 18, 1715, 'and agreed with Edw. Jenner to dig sandstone for setting up my father's tombstone, at 5s. I gave him 6d. to spend in drink, that he might be more careful.'

So much for the stone itself. When it came to the lettering, the evidence suggests that Marchant and his like either often failed to cough up the necessary beer money to ensure a thorough job (the basic rate at the time was a penny a word) or, conversely, that they provided rather too much of it: errors abound on our early memorials.

We should sympathise with the mason given the task of chiselling Ann More's gravestone which now sits inside the church tower at Wivelsfield, since he was asked to tackle a hefty chunk of Latin – but at what stage in the operation, we're prompted to ask, was the Latin introduced? The epitaph asks us, in translation, to remember:

Let's start again, please: when the mason made a slip in his Latin on Ann More's epitaph at Wivelsfield, he turned the stone upside down and had another go.

Ann, the wife of Elyott More, arms bearer, daughter of Edward Paine of East Grinstead, arms bearer, who died 12th December AD 1691 aged 43. We relinquish with pain those we truly love.

Turn the page upside down and you'll see that the mason began in common or garden English until he reached the word for 'arms bearer', which he, or his mentor, got wrong. The decision was then taken to put the whole epitaph into Latin, and the poor craftsman – no doubt calculating his potential loss if he forked out for a new stone – seems to have taken the easy way out and simply turned it round and begun

at the other end. After all, the mistake would be hidden when it was pushed down into the ground. But how jinxed the poor fellow seems to have been! Alongside the stone is another which (that damn Latin again) has been irretrievably ruined. Let's hope that he was forgiven.

A classic case of crude and ignorant stone carving can be enjoyed at East Dean in West Sussex *(next page)*, where the mason makes a memorable mess of William Peachey's headstone. The skull and crossbones at the top are wonderfully unmenacing, the spelling is atrocious and several of the words are uncomfortably broken:

> *HERE LYETH*
> *THE BODY OF W*
> *ILIAM PEACHE*
> *Y OF EASTDEAN*
> *BLACKSMITHW*
> *HO DISECASEDTH*
> *FEBBRUARY YE*
> *AOM DOM*

The letter *S* is uniformly reversed and an abortive attempt to begin the date at the end of the sixth line (a *TH* which comes to nothing) is quite forgotten by the end of the seventh. Although spelling was still fluid at this period (Dr Johnson's dictionary wasn't to appear until 1755), the *Wiliam* and *Febbruary* are obviously wrong, while *disecased* for 'deceased' is a truly exotic creation.

But what of the last line? The mason obviously had a notion that something rather like *AOM DOM* was usually carved at the foot of a stone (actually *Anno Domini*, for 'in the year of our Lord'), but he couldn't for the life of him quite remember how it went.

And did he know what it meant? It's quite possible that he did, but that he found himself too near the foot of his (Sussex marble) stone for comfort and therefore felt obliged to squeeze it above the bones at the top: *1688*. It remains a possibility, however that he hadn't a clue about its significance and thought he had done enough simply to carve the abbreviation. We shouldn't expect anything but the most basic standards of literacy from a country craftsman at this period.

At Wadhurst an epitaph on one of the notable iron graveslabs inside the church ends abruptly with the words *aetatis suae* ('at the age of'), the craftsman dutifully nodding towards convention but having no inkling that he really ought to find an appropriate figure to add.

There are 31 iron graveslabs at

William Peachey's gravestone at East Dean in West Sussex.

Wadhurst, dating from 1617 until 1799, during which period the area was an important centre of the prosperous Wealden iron industry. If the workmanship sometimes appears a little slipshod, the manufacturing process did demand concentration. The molten iron was poured into a frame on a bed of sand into which the letters *in reverse* had already been pressed – either separately or as a solid wooden block carved with the required epitaph, armorial bearings and so on. Sometimes the letters seem to have been simply scratched into the sand with a handy stick.

Once the iron had solidified, it would be turned over, the block removed and the sand brushed off. It's not at all difficult to imagine a careless craftsman absent-mindedly carving or placing one or two of the letters the wrong way round, and this is exactly what we find at Mayfield *(right)*. It's a mistake that could have been rectified only by recasting the entire slab.

Bad spelling, as several memorials in this book testify, is not confined to the days before dictionaries. The luckier culprit has his errors overlooked for being in an inconspicuous place (or, many years later, for being overgrown with moss and lichen), whereas other mistakes seem to leap out at you from the stone. At Hurstpierpoint, in the epitaph to Jane Smith – who died in 1867 at the age of 38 – we lament an, alas, all too 'inexpressible greif'. Was it noticed at the time?

It is hardly surprising, in a period of diminishing literacy, that we should find errors still being made today. Sometimes, unbeknown to the epitaph writers, a note of unintentional comedy is introduced.

A collector's item is to be found close to the tapsell gate at Jevington. The mason certainly can't be blamed for the infelicitous 'wiping out' imagery, which is truly dreadful, but he should really have known better than to give us 'all together' as one

Working back-to-front and right-to-left made life confusing for the maker of this iron graveslab *(above and below)* in the church at Mayfield.

word. As it is, we either ask ourselves 'altogether *what*?' or imagine that in their last days the husband and his dear departed wife were mentally, as one might say, a few ashes short of an urn:

THE YEARS MAY WIPE OUT MANY THINGS,
BUT YOU, THEY WIPE OUT NEVER.
THE MEMORY OF THOSE HAPPY DAYS
WHEN WE WERE ALTOGETHER.

'They that go down to the sea in ships . . .'

Memorials to master mariner Horatio Culston (died 1932) at Sidlesham *(left)* and to mariner Daniel Hack (died 1770) at West Wittering.

A PRIDE IN THE JOB

Periwinkle! Periwinkle!
Was ever her cry
She laboured to live
Poor and honest to die.
At the last day again
Her old eyes will twinkle!
For no more will they say
Periwink, Periwinkle!

The days when the labours of a simple winkle-seller earned a place on her gravestone, as Mary Atkinson's did in the grounds of Chichester Cathedral in 1786, are long gone – and to our loss. But our churchyards are well stocked with reminders of men and women who took a pride in their work and wished to be remembered for it.

Mariners

Whether Daniel Hack perished at sea isn't clear from his epitaph, though this 'faithful Servant' was only 30 when he died in 1770. The carving of a ship on the top of his headstone *(facing page)* isn't as fine as the one on Thomas Barrow's memorial at Bosham *(p. 28)*, but the wording is almost identical – another reminder of how lines were commonly borrowed and amended:

Tho Boreas's storms and Neptune's Waves
Have tos'd me to and fro
In spite of both by God's decree
I'm harboured here below
Where I do now at anchor lie
With many of our Fleet
But once again I must set sail
Our Saviour Christ to meet.

A handsome, and much more recent, red granite headstone at Sidlesham *(facing page)* remembers master mariner Horatio Sterney Culston, 'younger brother of Trinity House', who died in October 1932 at the age of 45. The lines at its foot are taken from Psalm 107:

THEY THAT GO DOWN TO THE SEA IN SHIPS
THAT DO BUSINESS IN GREAT WATERS
THESE SEE THE WORKS OF THE LORD
AND HIS WONDERS IN THE DEEP.

A glover

Fletching church contains several notable memorials (and Edward Gibbon, author of *The Decline and Fall of the Roman Empire*, is buried in the Sheffield Mausoleum), but the most unusual is the brass to Peter Denot. The pair of fashionable gloves at its foot marks his trade.

Denot was one of the many East Sussex men who, having joined Jack Cade's rebellion in 1450, were later pardoned – and so fine a memorial suggests that the episode left no indelible stain upon his character.

Peter Denot's memorial in Fletching church.

A dyer

A pun typical of the period suggests Adrian Stoughton's line of business on his monument of 1635 in the church at West Stoke:

> Death could not wound him, only clos'd
> his eye
> And made him dye to live that liv'd to dye.

The monument shows Stoughton, MP for Chichester, kneeling with his wife above their children: they had 16, nine of whom died in infancy.

Brewers

The Flemish brewer Derrick Carver was the first Protestant to be martyred during the reign of Bloody Queen Mary, and has a plaque in Brighton *(see page 77)*. Another Flemish brewer has a more

Flemish brewer's graveslab at Playden.

substantial memorial at Playden: a black stone slab of around 1530 which depicts two casks with a crossed fork and mash-stick. These were originally inlaid with brass. The beautifully worked inscription reads:

> Hier is begraven Cornelis
> Roetmans bidt voer de ziele.

This translates as 'Here lies Cornelis Roetmans. Pray for his soul.'

Thomas Tipper's eloquent epitaph at Newhaven (written by his, and Thomas Paine's, eccentric friend Clio Rickman) refers to the 'Stingo' which George IV enjoyed tippling. Tipper, who died in 1785 at the age of 54, had helped finance a drawbridge over the Ouse, and an engraving of it appears *(facing page)* at the top of the stone:

> Reader, with kind regard this Grave survey,
> Nor heedless pass where TIPPER'S ashes
> lay,
> Honest he was, ingenuous, blunt, and kind;
> And dared to, what few dare do, speak
> his mind.
> PHILOSOPHY and HISTORY well he knew,
> Was versed in PHYSICK and in SURGERY
> too.
> The best old STINGO he both brewed
> and sold;
> Nor did one knavish act to get his Gold.
> He played through Life a varied comic part,
> And knew immortal HUDIBRAS by heart.
> Reader, in real truth, such was the Man;
> Be better, wiser, laugh more if you can.

Mrs Gamp, in Dickens's *Martin Chuzzlewit*, is wont to take 'a pint of the celebrated staggering ale, or Real Old Brighton Tipper, at supper,' and tells a chambermaid: 'If they draws the Brighton Tipper here, I likes *that* ale at night, my love; it bein' considered wakeful by the doctors.'

Thomas Tipper's headstone at Newhaven.

A schoolmaster

Francis Howlett, the first schoolmaster at Hailsham about whom anything is known – 'comedian, schoolmaster, postmaster, tax collector, vestry clerk, printer, travelling librarian, musician and general referee', in the words of a friend – has a wooden leaping board in the churchyard which borrows a few lines from Goldsmith's *The Deserted Village*. He died in 1831 at the grand old age of 80:

There in the former vestry, skilled to rule,
The Village Master taught his little school
But past is all his fame, the very spot
Where many a time he triumphed is forgot.

A huntsman

Charlton, near Chichester, was famous for its hunt during the eighteenth century, attracting the aristocracy in their droves. One of the huntsmen, Tom Johnson, was such a legend in his own lifetime that when he died, in 1774, he warranted a substantial memorial inside the church at nearby Singleton. The chief part of the epitaph praises him in grandiloquent language, but it's the verse at the foot which lingers in the memory:

Here JOHNSON lies. What Hunter can deny
Old honest TOM the Tribute of a Sigh.
Deaf is the Ear, which caught the
opening Sound,
Dumb is the Tongue, which cheard the
Hills around.
Unpleasing Truth Death hunts us from our
Birth
In view, and Men, like foxes, take to Earth.

Wooden memorial to Francis Howlett, popular schoolmaster, at Hailsham.

Blacksmiths

William Stone, the Felpham blacksmith, died on January 17, 1808, and was given an epitaph that can be found elsewhere in Sussex and beyond:

> My sledge and hammer lie reclin'd
> My bellows too have lost their wind
> My fire extinct my forge decay'd
> And in the dust my vice is laid.
> My coal is spent my Iron gone
> My Nails are driven my work is done.

John Hammond (1911-1978), the village blacksmith at Offham, near Lewes, has an anvil decoration (*right, above*) on his headstone at Hamsey.

A carpenter

Mark Sharp's footstone at St John sub Castro, Lewes, shows his carpenter's tools.

Mark Sharp, who died in 1747, has a fine memorial in the churchyard of St John sub Castro, ('below the castle') at Lewes. His headstone (*page 8*) portrays a lively resurrection scene, while the footstone (*above*) depicts the tools of his trade. Fellow carpenters may spot, among other things, an axe, saw, jack plane, mallet and bevel.

Headstones to *(left)* a blacksmith at Hamsey, and *(below)* a jockey at Burpham.

Jockeys

The gravestone of a jockey is propped against the church wall at Burpham, his mount spurred on by a use of the whip which would surely have earned him disqualification today. Benjamin Brewster died in 1789, at the age of 47:

> Great grief and pain I under went
> Till my Blessd Lord he for me sent
> Weep not my wife be satisfyd
> We prayd for Life but GOD denyd.

Terence Redding (1946-1971), buried at Clayton, has a verse which alludes to his line of work:

> And when the starting gate sprang wide
> To launch you in the great unknown . . .

Another jockey is remembered up on the old Lewes racecourse:

> THIS IS TO MARK
> THE BURIAL PLACE OF
> SHAUN SPADAH
> WINNER OF THE GRAND NATIONAL IN
> 1921
> AND OF THE ASHES OF
> F.B. REES
> HIS JOCKEY, WHICH WERE AT HIS WISH
> SCATTERED HERE IN 1951.

Farmers

Our farmers may leave a landscape behind them, but they have their fixed memorials, too. At West Burton, Fred Hughes of Southover Farm has his epitaph not in a churchyard but close to a public footpath which looks down on the land he tilled. (There's a wooden seat close by, for the benefit of walkers.) Fred was something of an individualist, which explains the line about freedom. His wife, Winifred, was a kindly soul who, in a poem, urged readers to smile at anyone they met, since this might well be 'someone you could put your arms around':

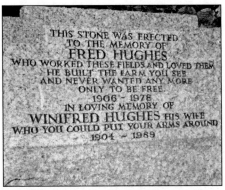

At West Burton Fred and Winifred Hughes have a memorial overlooking their farm.

THIS STONE WAS ERECTED
TO THE MEMORY OF
FRED HUGHES
WHO WORKED THESE FIELDS AND
LOVED THEM
HE BUILT THE FARM YOU SEE
AND NEVER WANTED ANY MORE
ONLY TO BE FREE.
1906-1978
IN LOVING MEMORY OF
WINIFRED HUGHES HIS WIFE
WHO YOU COULD PUT YOUR ARMS
AROUND
1904-1989.

A corn merchant

Farmers are sometimes given the carving of a wheatsheaf on their headstones, and the same motif can be seen at Crawley on either side of the memorial to the local corn merchant Moses Nightingale, who died in 1934.

A dipper

In Georgian times, when the 'quality' first came to Brighton to swim in the salt sea (and to drink it) for their health, the gentlemen were plunged into the water by 'bathers' and the ladies by 'dippers'. Martha Gunn, 'Queen of the Dippers', was buried in St Nicholas's churchyard, Brighton, after giving prodigiously long service:

In memory of
STEPHEN GUNN
who died 4th of september, 1813,
Aged 79 Years
Also MARTHA, Wife of
STEPHEN GUNN
Who was Peculiarly Distinguished as a
bather in this Town nearly 70 Years
She died 2nd of May, 1815,
Aged 88 Years.

Martha Gunn was a favourite of the Prince of Wales, who granted her free access to the grand kitchen of the Royal Pavilion, so it's fitting that she should have another kind of memorial in the Pavilion itself – a portrait by John Russell, warts (or plumpness) and all.

A wheelwright

The Woolgar family owned forges and wheelwright businesses in Upper Beeding, Bramber, Steyning and Storrington. Charles Woolgar was a member of the Guild of Sussex Craftsmen. His headstone at Steyning (shared with his wife and 18-year-old son) has a wheel decoration at the foot and declares proudly:

He was a wright.

Entertainers

Anna Maria Crouch, the famous 19th century actress, is buried in St Nicholas churchyard, Brighton, her tomb made of Coadestone and surmounted by a large urn. Her epitaph makes no attempt to stint her praise:

She combined with the purest taste as a singer
the most elegant simplicity as an Actress
beautiful almost beyond parallel in her Person.
She was distinguished by the powers of her
mind
they enabled her when she had quitted the
stage
to gladden the life by the charms of her
conversation and refine it by her manners.

Robert Newell died in 1750 at the age of 79, and is buried at North Stoke. A verse on his floorslab in the chancel suggests that he, too, was an actor:

Grown ripe in vertue at a good old age
It pleased the Lord to call him of ye stage.

G.H. Elliott, buried at Rottingdean in 1962, performed under a stage name which would be unimaginable today. His gravestone shows a stage with the curtains drawn back:

The last curtain call for
G.H. ELLIOTT
The Chocolate Coloured Coon

Next to Elliott's plot is the grave of Lal Cliff, 'coon singer and dancer' (1884-1962) and her husband, the music hall artist Harry Bamford (1883-1973). The stone is inscribed at the top with a Shakespearian reference: 'All the world is a stage, and I one of its players.'

The *what*? Yes, G.H. Elliott, buried at Rottingdean, was known as The Chocolate Coloured Coon.

EVER FAITHFUL

Against the east wall of the church at Herstmonceux is a tombstone which carries an epitaph whose sentiments are entirely of this world:

> Near this place lieth interred
> the Body of Richard Morris
> who died the 21st day of July 1749
> aged 63 years,
> who himself desired it might be
> remembered that he owed his Bread
> to his Grace the Duke of Newcastle
> his great Benefactor.

It would have been a kindness, surely, had the grand duke penned a line or two in return, praising poor Richard, however humble his station. Such an action would not have been out of place, for there are, fortunately, several instances of the well-to-do raising memorials to those who have served them well.

There could scarcely be a tribute more generous than the one to be found on a now only partially legible tablet at Petworth:

> In Memory
> of SARAH BETTS, widow,
> who passed nearly 50 Years in one Service
> and died January 2, 1792
> Aged 75.
> Farewell! dear Servant! since thy heavenly Lord
> Summons thy worth to its supreme reward.
> Thine was a spirit that no toil could tire,
> "When Service sweat for duty, not for hire."
> From him whose childhood cherished by thy care,
> Weathered long years of sickness and despair,
> Take what may haply touch the best above,
> Truth's tender praise! and tears of grateful love.

A haunting image at Wivelsfield – the faces of children peeping through the leaves of a tree – in memory of a beloved nanny.

Lovely! But a modern memorial in the churchyard at Wivelsfield (by Hilary Stratton, a former apprentice of Eric Gill), matches it for tenderness. It remembers Jessie Edey (1885-1969), who served one family as nanny for more than half a century. The wording is affectingly simple:

> DEAR MOOSE
> DEVOTED HER LIFE WITH LOVE AND
> LOYALTY TO OTHER PEOPLE'S
> CHILDREN

and, a haunting touch, the headstone has the carving of an oak tree with three of her little charges peeking out from between the branches. Vida Herbison, seen as a four-year-old in the centre of the tree, explains the oak: 'English through and through, and that's what Moose was. And don't call her a servant – she was *family*!'

At Laughton, the chancel was rebuilt and refurbished by the mighty Pelhams (Earls of Chichester) to become, in effect, their chantry, with the family vault beneath. A plaque set into the outside wall speaks of a servant's utter devotion – and offers us a comically literal notion of togetherness at the Resurrection:

ANN LUND
DIED AT STANMER IN FEBRUARY 1839
AGED 70.
DURING MANY YEARS OF FAITHFUL
SERVICE UNDER THE 2ND
AND 3RD EARLS OF CHICHESTER HER
DEVOTED ATTACHMENT,
HER CONSISTENT PIETY AND HER SELF
DENYING CHARITY
GAINED FOR HER THE RESPECT AND
LOVE OF ALL WHO KNEW HER.
HER REMAINS ARE DEPOSITED TO THE
SOUTH OF THIS STONE IN
COMPLIANCE WITH HER EXPRESSED
WISH
THAT HER BODY MIGHT RISE
AT THE LAST WITH THOSE OF THE
FAMILY SHE SO DEARLY LOVED.

Can we not visualise old Ann reaching out a desperate hand to clutch the robes of her ladyship on her way to heaven?

Long service features on a wooden board at Cuckfield, originally erected in 1840 and since renewed:

This Rail is placed by Mr SERGISON to the memory of SARAH TULET, who died at Cuckfield Place March 9th 1840, in the 78th Year of her age, having served in the Family with the strictest Fidelity, Honesty and Sobriety for upwards of Fifty Years.
"Be thou faithful unto Death and I will give thee a Crown of Life."

Gardeners might have been included in the 'trades & professions' chapter of this book, but in the heyday of the great estates they were part of a large family enterprise, and were valued accordingly – although the word 'servitude' sits rather unhappily on an epitaph at Fletching:

In memory of Richard Simmons, who (after a servitude of nearly 50 years as under gardener at Sheffield Park in this parish) departed this life 26th October 1850, aged 75 years.

'Fidelity, Honesty & Sobriety': a valued servant at Cuckfield.

The headstone of Ernest Hayes at Cuckfield was paid for by his employer:

IN LOVING MEMORY
OF
ERNEST STANLEY HAYES
DEAREST HUSBAND OF
ELIZABETH HAYES
DIED MAY 5TH 1956
AGED 66 YEARS

THIS STONE WAS ERECTED
BY
ERNEST G. KLEINWORT
IN GRATEFUL APPRECIATION OF 21
YEARS
OF DEVOTED SERVICE AS HEAD
GARDENER
AT HEASELANDS, CUCKFIELD.

Servants were evidently held in high esteem at Chailey, since there are no fewer than eleven headstones to them in a relatively small churchyard, several, including that of Henry Carvill (the surname is difficult to decipher), erected by the same family. It's good to know – few epitaphs tell us this – that Henry had the luck to go peacefully:

Here lieth the body of
HENRY CARVILL
who was found dead in his bed
at the Hook the 11th March 1871
aged 62 years
having died apparently without a struggle.

Arguably the weirdest Christian name on any Sussex tombstone is to be found at Uckfield:

SACRED
TO THE MEMORY OF
NAPKIN BROOKER
WHO DIED
APRIL THE 4TH 1862
AGED 91 YEARS

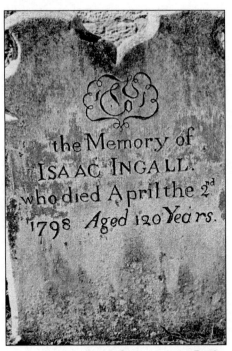

An ancient servant at Battle.

He was, the epitaph goes on to say, 'for 53 years a faithful and respected servant on the Rocks estate', but how did he get such an arresting monicker? He was apparently a foundling – left swaddled in nothing more than a large napkin.

For length of service (or, indeed, for longevity) few can compare with the remarkable Isaac Ingall at Battle. He died on April 2, 1798, at the reputed age of 120, which is far and away a Sussex churchyard record, and he served as butler to the Webster family at Battle Abbey for all of 90 years.

The story goes that he fell out with his employers at the age of 90 and set out to walk to Hastings in search of new employment before being persuaded to stay.

Friends and enemies. The Chattri *(below),* on the Downs above Patcham, is a tribute to Indian soldiers 'who gave their lives in the services of their King Emperor in the Great War.' The obelisk *(left)* at St John sub Castro, Lewes, was raised in 1877 by Czar Alexander in honour of Finns who had been captured by the British during the Crimean War and who died while held in the Naval Prison at Lewes.

FOR GOD AND COUNTRY

A mystery at Steyning: what was so special about James Day?

There are so many memorials in Sussex to soldiers, sailors and airmen (not all of whom have lost their lives in war) that a rigorous selection is in order – and what stranger first entry than an epitaph to a plucky *woman* soldier? Phoebe Hessel disguised herself as a man in order to be with her soldier lover, and her memorial in St Nicholas's churchyard, Brighton, gives the outline of her life story. The poor mason, being given so much information to impart, reasoned that the best he could do with some lines was to omit the gaps between words altogether:

In Memory of
PHOEBE HESSEL
who was born at Stepney in the Year 1713
She served for many Years
as a private Soldier in the 5th Regt of foot
in different parts of Europe
andintheYear1745foughtunderthecommand
of the DUKE OF CUMBERLAND
at the Battle of Fontenoy
whereshereceivedaBayonetwoundinherArm
Her long life which commenced in the time of
QUEEN ANNE
extended to the reign of
GEORGE IV
bywhosemunificenceshereceivedcomfort
and support in her latter Years
shediedatBrightonwhereshehadlongresided
December 12th 1821 Aged 108 Years.

Her tale seems to have been greatly embroidered, but it did win her a royal half guinea a week for life.

Public sentiment has inspired the raising of many large memorials like those on the facing page, but the plain and simple often prove just as moving. What story, for instance, lies behind the stone to James Day at Steyning? We learn that he served in the North Hants Light Infantry and died on June 3, 1804, at the age of 21, but why, of all the soldiers buried here during the Napoleonic Wars, was young James singled out in this way?

James he is dead,is all his Comrades cry
And Grief was seen,in every light Bobs eye
*No more the Bugle horn to him shall soun*ᵈ
to hurry him over the furrowed Ground
But now alas his body lay at rest
In hopes his soul will be for everBlesst.
NB.this Stone was errected by his
Comrades,as a small tribute ofrespect
Due to a worthy Youth like him.

The verse is rather clumsy, the spelling and the execution erratic and the closing *NB* a decidedly awkward touch, but these little blemishes only increase the pathos.

Criticism of the military high command is rare on memorials to the fallen, but there's no mistaking the anger on the epitaph in Cuckfield church (under a flamboyantly homo-erotic death scene) to Captain Percy Burrell of the Sixth Regiment of Dragoon Guards, who was killed 'at the illconcerted and fatal attack on Buenos-Aires' on July 5, 1803:

WHILST IN THE ACT OF ENCOURAGING BY HIS INTREPID EXAMPLE THE EXERTIONS OF HIS MEN WHO WERE EXPOSED TO A MOST DESTRUCTIVE FIRE, HE WAS MORTALLY WOUNDED BY A MUSKET SHOT.

At Heathfield we find the monument as folly. Brigadier General George Augustus Elliott, who held the Rock of Gibraltar against a siege by French and Spanish forces between 1779 and 1783, is spendidly remembered in the grounds of his home, Heathfield Park. Three years after his death in 1792 the new owner (Francis Newbury, High Sheriff of Sussex) built a 55ft high, three-storey circular tower to commemorate his exploits. This folly has suffered from sorry neglect, but a sign over the door – the lettering said to have been made of metal from the guns of the Spanish floating batteries – still clearly reads *CALPES DEFENSORI*: 'To the defender of Gibraltar.'

To study the memorials of Sussex soldiers is to be aware of how many wars there have been over the past two centuries, and in how many far-flung places. At Tillington there's a memorial to a Peninsular War victim, John Ayling:

SLAIN IN THE TRENCHES BEFORE BADAJOS
23 YRS   6 APRIL 1812

Captain Percy Burrell's monument in Cuckfield church criticises the army command for its handling of the battle in which he was killed.

Twenty eight Finnish prisoners of the Crimean War died in Lewes *(page 48)*, while an English survivor of the same conflict is buried at West Chiltington. George Johnson's epitaph, which describes him as a 'Crimean veteran' (having been at the battle of Alma and the bombardment of Sebastopol), ends by suggesting that he had the reputation of being somewhat grumpy:

Behind a frowning countenance he hides a smiling face.

As for the most famous battle of the Crimean War, when hundreds of British soldiers died in a gallant but ill-timed attack on Russian artillery at Balaclava, Sussex has a notable connection. Martin Leonard Landfried, buried in the cemetery at Hove, was the young trumpeter who sounded the Charge of the Light Brigade on October 25, 1854.

There are more than a hundred names on the memorial in the Old Steine, Brighton, to soldiers killed on expeditions along the Nile in the 1880s. Some died at the Battle of Abu Klea in January 1885, when a British taskforce seeking to relieve General Gordon at Khartoum was attacked by twelve thousand 'whirling Dervishes'. Kipling wrote a poem about the battle ('So 'ere's to you, Fuzzy-Wuzzy, at your 'ome in the Sudan . . .') which now seems in very bad taste.

A survivor of the American War of Independence is remembered at Hurstpierpoint:

Sacred
to the memory of
WILLIAM FORTUNE
COLONEL COMMANDANT of
THE MILITIA OF SOUTH CAROLINA
in the American War
he departed this life on the 20th day of Novr
1822
in the 71st year
of his life.

Henry Holden, an Englishman, fought on the other side of the Atlantic, too, and won the Congressional Medal of Honor for his bravery when fighting alongside the ill-fated General Custer at the Battle of Little Big Horn.

His headstone in the Bear Road cemetery, Brighton, gives only the basic facts. Holden's company having been pinned down by five thousand Sioux and Cheyenne warriors, he risked his life by braving a hail of bullets to fetch ammunition from one of the pack horses. He died in Brighton in 1905 at the age of 69.

And to continue the American theme, the first American serviceman to die in the second world war, Pilot Officer Bill Fiske, is buried at Boxgrove. He was killed in action in 1940 while stationed at nearby Tangmere – where Allied and German servicemen lie together in the churchyard.

At Butts Brow, above Willingdon, is a stone which remembers some other American airmen:

In memory of the crew of a B-24D Liberator bomber No 41-24282 Bar Y "Ruth-Less"

506 Squaddron 44th Bombardment Group 8th U.S.A.A.F

Who all lost their lives, when damaged by enemy action and in very low cloud the aircraft crashed here on February 2nd 1944.

Our volunteers soldiers shouldn't be forgotten – and the monument to Captain Hans Buck at Frant ensure that they are not. He founded the Volunteer Army which was later to develop into the Territorial Army.

He fought with Custer at Little Big Horn: headstone at Brighton to Henry Holden.

51

An army cyclist's headstone at Broadwater Cemetery, with an unusual message at its foot. Whose darling *was* he?

The standard military headstone is a clean and dignified thing, with little variation save in the emblem at the top. Corporal H.C. Forrest's stone in Broadwater Cemetery is unusual in recording that he was a member of the Army Cyclist Corps (he died in December 1918, a few weeks after the signing of the armistice), but what leaps, rather shockingly, from the stone is the message at the foot:

GOOD NIGHT, DARLING

Some memorials are to be found in relatively remote places, marking the spot where the men died. On Crowborough Common, for instance, a monument remembers nine Canadian servicemen who were killed on July 5, 1944, while stationed there under canvas. Another memorial *(facing page)*, on Ashdown Forest and misleadingly known as 'the airmen's grave' (nobody is buried there), salutes six men who died when their Wellington bomber crashed while returning from a raid on the German city of Cologne:

To the glorious memory of Sgt/PVR Sutton, aged 24 years, 142 Bom. Sqdn. R.A.F., also his five comrades who lost their lives through enemy action.
31.7.41. Mother.

Another grieving mother had a small cross placed by the roadside at Dallington to honour her pilot son, shot down in a dogfight over Sussex during the Battle of Britain. Flying officer Peter Guerin Crofts, a nephew of the Commander-in-Chief Fighter Command, Air Chief Marshal Lord Dowding, baled out of his plane but lost his parachute. The cross, near Padgham Corner, has been renewed in recent years:

IN GRATEFUL REMEMBRANCE OF
PETER GUERIN CROFTS
FLYING OFFICER ROYAL AIR FORCE
WHO NEAR THIS SPOT GAVE HIS
LIFE IN THE BATTLE OF BRITAIN
ON SEPT 28TH 1940 AND IS ONE
OF THE FEW TO WHOM SO MANY
OWE SO MUCH

An airman's roadside cross at Dallington.

Douglas Arnold was a Spitfire pilot who survived the war – unlike Pilot Officer Gillespie Magee of the Royal Canadian Air Force, whose poem graces his memorial at West Grinstead:

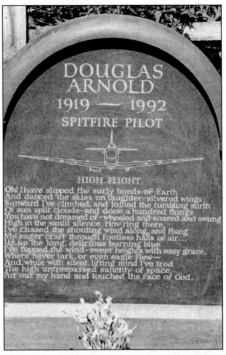

HIGH FLIGHT

Oh! I have slipped the surly bonds of Earth
And danced the skies on laughter-silvered
                                   wings:
Sunward I've climbed, and joined the
                            tumbling mirth
Of sun split clouds – and done a hundred things
You have not dreamed of – wheeled and
                    soared and swung
High in the sunlit silence. Hov'ring there
I've chased the shouting wind along, and flung
My eager craft through footless halls of air . . .
Up, up the long, delirious burning blue
I've topped the wind-swept heights with
                            easy grace,
Where never lark, or even eagle flew –
And, while with silent, lifting mind I've trod
The high untrespassed sanctity of space,
Put out my hand and touched the face of God.

A Spitfire pilot at West Grinstead.

The 'airmen's grave' on Ashdown Forest is, in fact, a memorial to Sgt Pilot Victor Sutton and his five companions, whose plane crashed here in July 1941.

Notable among memorials to our sailors is the plaque on the wall of the bell tower in Seaford church to James Walker, who died in 1831. He was, we learn, Rear Admiral of the Red – glorious title – and his epitaph has the rare flourish of an exclamation mark. He was:

> a most brave and distinguished officer who served, fought, and conquered with Rodney, Howe, Duncan, St Vincent and the immortal Nelson!

Admiral Walker's tomb in the northern corner of the churchyard carries a similar tribute, but without that rare 'screamer' at the end.

This is the place to note a couple of other Nelson connections. His sister is buried at Slaugham, while at Hove (in the carriage drive, near the west door) is the tomb of Admiral Sir George Westphal who, as a boy, was a midshipman on *HMS Victory* and was wounded at the Battle of Trafalgar.

To quote the church guide: 'He lay in the cockpit next to the dying Nelson, whose jacket was placed beneath the boy's bleeding head, and as it had adhered to the blood, it was necessary to cut away a portion of the epaulette from the Admiral's jacket in order to release the boy.'

Many years later, when Westphal himself had become a retired admiral, and was living in Hove, the Imperial Services Museum wrote to ask him if he could vouch for the genuineness of a jacket that had been offered to them as that of Nelson. He replied that if four tufts of the fringe of the epaulette were missing from the left shoulder it would be genuine: 'The jacket was purchased for the nation.'

A man of the same period and rank has an attractive memorial inside the church at Hartfield, including the bas-relief of a man of war:

SACRED
TO THE MEMORY OF
REAR ADMIRAL\
THE HON^{BLE} MAJOR JACOB HENNIKER
OF ASHDOWN PARK, IN THIS PARISH.
HE WAS
IN CONSTANT ACTIVE SERVICE IN
VARIOUS
PARTS OF THE GLOBE
FROM HIS FIRST ENTERING THE NAVY
IN 1794,
TO THE CLOSE OF THE WAR IN 1814,
AND DISTINGUISHED HIMSELF IN
SEVERAL ENGAGEMENTS.
HE DIED JUNE 5TH 1843,
LEAVING A NUMEROUS FAMILY
TO MOURN HIS IRREPARABLE LOSS.

British man-of-war on a rear admiral's memorial in Hartfield church.

GRIPES AND GRIEVANCES

Most epitaphs strive to give the dead a comfortable send-off, with praise for past triumphs or hopes for the future, but occasionally we come across simmering resentments, smouldering anger, unfinished business. The cause of the ill-feeling is sometimes obscure, sometimes patently obvious.

Walter Budd's gravestone at Dragons Green manages to give 'the enemy' one in the eye twice over: through its wording and its situation. Walter, an albino and an epileptic, lived with his parents at the George and Dragon pub. It seems that he was treated unkindly by some of the locals, and in 1893, after being accused of a trivial theft, he drowned himself. He was 26 years old.

His parents arranged to have him buried in the churchyard at Shipley, a few miles away, but when the vicar read the wording they had devised for the gravestone he refused to accept it:

May God forgive those who forgot their duty to him who was just and afflicted.

Walter's parents, resisting any suggestion that they should alter the offending words, had the memorial installed instead at a spot where it would be noticed far more readily by those for whom the criticism was intended – in the front garden of their pub. It still stands there today.

Isaac Allen, buried at Lindfield, thought himself very badly treated, as his brass, set into the chancel floor, declares.

HERE LYETH INTERRED YE BODY OF ISAAC ALLEN ONLY SONNE OF ABRAHAM ALLEN ESQ BY HIS WIFE JOANE LOVE HEE DYED AT LONDON, A PRISONER TO YE UPPER-BENCH, UPON AN ACCON FOR WORDES, MOST FALSELY & MALICIOUSLY, BY ONE SINGLE WITNESS SWORNE AGAINST HIM, AS HE HAD OFTEN-TYMES, & ON HIS DEATH-BED PROTESTED & DECLARED TO SEVERALL FRIENDS. HEE DESIRED HIS BODY MIGHT BEE BURYED HERE AT LINFEILD NEARE HIS MOTHER, & DECEACED YE 24TH DAY OF JULY ANº DONI 1656 AGED 63.

What Allen was accused of we don't know, but his brass is interesting for its use of the term 'upper-bench': he was imprisoned during the time of Cromwell's Commonwealth, and in those levelling days the customary name 'King's Bench' wasn't used.

Walter Budd's gravestone was erected in a pub garden after the vicar refused to have it in Shipley churchyard.

A legal claim seems to have been promoted on an iron graveslab to Anne Forster at Crowhurst, which was copied and used for firebacks all over Sussex. This, incidentally, is one for the 'many a slip' collection, with every *S* and *F* resolutely upside-down:

> HER:LIETH:ANE:FORST
> R:DAUGHTER:AND:
> HEYR:TO:THOMAS:
> GAYNSFORD:ESQUIER
> DECEASED:XVIII:OF
> JANUARY:1591:LEAVYNG
> BEHIND:HER:II: SONES:
> AND:V:DAUGHTERS.

It's just possible that the ironmaster concerned was merely saving himself money by using the one graveslab template for a number of firebacks, in which case it must have seemed an unusual design, to say the least. A better guess, perhaps, is that those concerned with establishing the rights of Anne's two sons and five daughters embarked on a cunning publicity campaign on their behalf – the spin doctors of their time. Unhappily we don't know whether their ploy was successful.

Copies of Anne Forster's iron graveslab (this one in Anne of Cleve's House, Lewes) were used as firebacks all over Sussex. Was someone eager to make a legal point?

There's no mistaking the bitterness of Anne Croker's epitaph at West Chiltington *(opposite page)*. On the face of it she was tolerably well connected, but her memorial makes it clear that she had to put up with some unpleasant legal sniping:

> In memory of ANNE late
> wife of JAMES CROKER A.M.
> Rector of Sullington and
> Daug^r of THO^s OSBORNE
> Esqr of Newtember in Sussex
> by a lawful wife. She Died
> August 14 1744 Aged 38.
> There the Wicked cease from
> troubling & there ye weary
> be at rest Job 3, !7
> Now perjury and forgery
> can hurt no longer.

Someone, presumably, had set about denying Anne her birthright, but whether she managed to prove her title before she died we don't know.

A disdainful waspishness is given off by the epitaph of Charles Sergison *(see page 17),* who is buried at Cuckfield. Sergison, who lived at Cuckfield Place, served for many years as MP for New Shoreham, and in 1671, we learn, was 'initiated into ye Civil Government of the Royal Navy':

> and laudably served through several Offices till the Year 1719 (namely 48 Years) 35 of which as a Principal Officer and Commissioner, to the satisfaction of the several Kings and Queens, and their greatest Ministers, and all his Superiors, about which time the Civil Government of the Navy being put into Military hands, he was esteemed by them, not a fit person to serve any longer.

In other words, what bloody fools they were to deprive themselves of his invaluable services.

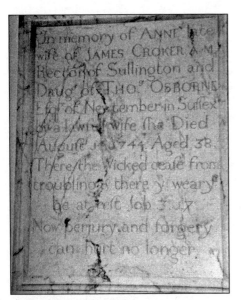

'Now perjury and forgery can hurt no longer': a bitter memorial in the church at West Chiltington.

The tribute to Thomas Eades in his church at Chiddingly, while it certainly takes a dig at his foes, has far more dignity. He was a non-juror, one of those beneficed clergy who refused to take the oath of allegiance to the Protestant William and Mary after the Glorious Revolution of 1689. The writer of his epitaph scores a point or two on his behalf:

The body of Mr Thomas Eades lies here,
A faithful shepherd that did not power fear,
But kept old Truth and would not let him go,
Nor turn out of the way for friend or foe.
He was suspended in the Dutchman's days,
Because he would not walk in their strange ways.

In the chancel at Wadhurst is a floor slab to the Rev. James Wilcocke, which also strikes a sharp blow for the old religion. Wilcocke, who died in 1660, two years after the Restoration, was 'intruded' upon the church – that is, forced upon a reluctant parish during Cromwell's Commonwealth because he was prepared to take services with a Puritan flavour. Perhaps the writer of his epitaph thought he was on safe ground if he expressed himself in Latin; perhaps he knew that nobody would object in any case.

The epitaph begins, the adjective spanning the lines :

JACOBUS WILCOCKE INDIGNISSI
MUS HUJUS LOCI MINISTER

This translates as: *John Wilcocke, most unworthy minister of this place.*

Occasionally we find expressions of triumph over the foe. At Tillington a brass plate records what's claimed as a great victory by the Rev Dr William Cox – an outspoken royalist during the Commonwealth – in a debate with the Puritan theologian Fisher. The Latin script calls him 'a protector of the orthodox faith' and adds that 'he suffered indignities at the hands of the rebels because of his unswerving loyalty to the king'. In fact, he so hated the 'rantings' of the rector of Petworth (where he lived) that he had himself buried at Tillington instead. The epitaph describes the debate as if it were a bout of all-in wrestling:

Descending into the arena against the anti-
infant-baptism brawler, Fisher, this vigorous
athlete prevailed gloriously at the parish church
of Petworth in the year of salvation 1654.

At Broadwater, now hidden by tiles under the communion table, is the tomb of Edward Burton, who was chaplain to Charles the First and later rector here. The epitaph pulls no ecclesiastical punches:

He was always a hater and smiter of the
Presbyterians.

IN MEMORY OF
WARRIOR BIRDS
WHO GAVE THEIR LIVES ON ACTIVE SERVICE 1939~45
AND FOR THE USE AND PLEASURE OF LIVING BIRDS.

Only in England . . .

The memorial to heroic wartime carrier pigeons in Beach House Park, Worthing.

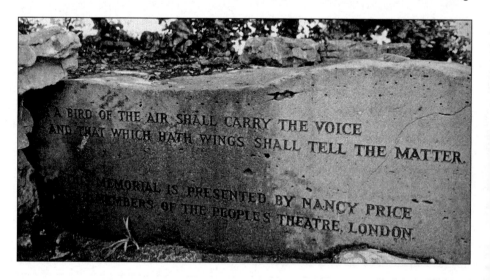

A BIRD OF THE AIR SHALL CARRY THE VOICE
AND THAT WHICH HATH WINGS SHALL TELL THE MATTER.

THIS MEMORIAL IS PRESENTED BY NANCY PRICE
MEMBERS OF THE PEOPLES THEATRE, LONDON.

ANIMAL SPIRITS

Set within shrubbery on a large mound in Beach House Park, Worthing, is the ultimate testimony to the British love of animals. Two stones by a pool *(facing page)* carry tributes to carrier pigeons killed in action:

IN MEMORY OF
WARRIOR BIRDS
WHO GAVE THEIR LIVES ON ACTIVE SERVICE
1939-45
AND FOR THE USE AND PLEASURE OF LIVING
BIRDS.

A BIRD OF THE AIR SHALL CARRY THE VOICE
AND THAT WHICH HATH WINGS SHALL TELL
THE MATTER

THIS MEMORIAL IS PRESENTED BY NANCY
PRICE
AND MEMBERS OF THE PEOPLE'S THEATRE,
LONDON.

The quotation, for the record, is from the Book of Ecclesiastes.

If this seems a touch eccentric, we should note that a carrier pigeon was awarded the Dicky Medal for bravery in battle. Nancy Price, the writer who paid for this memorial, lived close to High Salvington windmill which was used as an ARP animals' centre during the war, even having its own ambulance.

Illustrations of animals on headstones are not uncommon, especially by the graves of young children, but for their actual memorials we have to look beyond our churchyards. There are certainly vicars who will conduct a remembrance service for a beloved pet, but fully-fledged funerals are not allowed – whether our dumb friends have souls remains a moot point – and the only way to have an animal interred in holy ground is (an extreme step) to arrange for it to be put down at the time of its owner's death so that it may share the plot.

Our obsession with animals can at times verge on the ludicrous. A colleague of mine would, when she moved house, dig up the bones of her former cats in order to take them with her, until a flat with nothing but window boxes at last (I *think*) defeated her.

Horses, unless cremated, do pose something of a space problem, but several, nonetheless, have been given the full treatment of burial and a headstone. We noticed a Grand National winner at Lewes *(p. 42)*: another, the famous Aldaniti – who won the race in 1981 after overcoming serious injuries, and was ridden by Bob Champion, himself freshly recovered from cancer – is buried at Nick Embiricos' Kirdford stud farm where he died in March, 1997, and a small plaque marks the spot.

A horse owned by the disgraced financier Horatio Bottomley was buried close to the racecourse he developed next to his house at Upper Dicker, and the stone can be seen in the grounds of Clifton Farmshop.

An imposing 40ft high mound topped by a stone toadstool in the gardens of the old manor house at Eastbourne (now the Towner Art Gallery) is inscribed with the words:

GRANITE JANUARY 1 1886.

No, nothing to do with the material, but the name of another favourite steed, which is buried here. On a lawn near the house there are several other animal graves, including one to a dog:

Duke, February 1912

Colonel Jack Colvin of the 9th Lancers was so enamoured of the horse which carried him through the first world war that he buried it in the grounds of his house at Partridge Green (flanking the recreation ground), with a substantial headstone recording his gratitude. Hopit's hooves were *not* buried, but saved as family mementoes: inkwell, doorstop, candle-holders:

HOPIT
B.G. BY POPOF
DAM BY NOBLE CHIEFTAIN 1904
SERVED THROUGHOUT THE GREAT WAR
AS CHARGER TO LIEUT JOHN FORRESTER
COLVIN, QUEEN'S ROYAL LANCERS
2 NOV. 1914 TO 11 NOV. 1918:
ARMY OF OCCUPATION OF THE RHINE
1918-1919
DIED JAN 7, 1927.

In the south-western corner of the old walled garden at Preston Manor (with access from Preston Park), is a pets'

cemetery. The family which once owned the manor buried their dogs and cats here, and the tradition continued (this is the last resting place of a town hall cat, no less) after the manor was taken over by Brighton Council.

Dogs' graves abound in Sussex, and several can be found along the ridge of the South Downs – where, presumably, their inhabitants used to bound and scamper. In Larkin's Field, Eastbourne, on the western boundary with Compton Place Road, stands a memorial stone to one who served, unofficially, with the army:

HERE LIES
HARLEQUIN
PET FOXHOUND OF THE
9TH SERVICE BATTN
THE BORDER REGT
(PIONEERS)
RUN OVER BY A MOTOR CAR
AND KILLED
21ST FEBRUARY 1915

Every dog, and cat, must have its day – and there's a last resting place for them at Preston Manor, Brighton.

TRULY MEMORABLE

So strange are some of the epitaphs reported by earlier writers that any new researcher must harbour the reluctant suspicion that they may be apocryphal. To come across Richard Turner's at Lindfield, however, is to scatter such notions to the wind: anything is possible; nothing, however bizarre, should be discounted.

The first three lines can be found, with variations, all over the country. But that wonderful ending! Richard was evidently an amputee, but who can hold back a smile at the irrelevance of it, the swooping bathos? An extra triumph is the use of 'fust', a rare example of a dialect word on our Sussex headstones. The lettering was recut by John Skelton in the 1950s:

'My Leg and Thigh was buried fust'. This strange epitaph for an amputee at Lindfield contains a rare example of a dialect word on a headstone.

In
Memory of
RICHARD TURNER
who DIED November 13th
1768 Aged 21 Years

Long was my Pain, great was my Grief
Surgeons I'd many but no Relief
I trust through Christ to rise with the just
My Leg and Thigh was buried fust.

A posthumous prize for the worst rhyme of all (though there are many contenders) should probably be awarded to the Arundel mason responsible for an epitaph now, I think, completely worn away:

In memory of
Elizabeth, Wife of
NATHAN PLEAS
Who on the 10th of July 1769
Her soul to God she did resign.
With Illness long she was perplex'd
Until her age was Sixty-six.

This miscellaneous chapter inevitably asks more questions than it can answer. Who, for example, was the man remembered (although now long forgotten) on a small headstone in St Anne's churchyard, Lewes?

Here Lieth
the Body of Litle
BENJAMIN
the Ruler died
Aug. 21, 1747, Aged 89.

It has been variously suggested that he may have been a jockey or a gipsy, but his name doesn't appear in the church register, and he has never been identified. In 1719 there was a churchwarden in the parish named Benjamin Ellis, but there is no other clue. And why 'Ruler'?

A rescued slave

One would love to know more about the remarkably named Tom M.S. Highflyer, buried at Woodvale, Brighton. It wasn't, of course, his real name. We can only envisage a frightened, dark-skinned little boy shivering on the deck of a small vessel in the Arabian sea as a British boat draws near – the MS Highflyer, presumably.

At least his cross gives us a few facts to work on:

IN MEMORY OF
TOM M.S. HIGHFLYER
RESCUED FROM A SLAVE DHOW
AUGUST 24 1866
BAPTISED BY HIS OWN REQUEST AT
BRIGHTON
MARCH 30 1870
DIED AT BRIGHTON JUNE 20, 1870
SUPPOSED TO BE ABOUT 12 YEARS OLD.

One that got away: epitaph at Cuckfield.

Sports & pastimes

Let's hope, for the sake of Richard Pippard *(above)* and Alban Barchard *(below)* that the world hereafter has rivers teeming with fish and at least one well-mown field suitable for a set of stumps and a sightscreen. The simple message 'Gone fishing' will seem flippant to some, but we may assume that it was as much a part of Pippard's life as the trades which some

'Rescued from a slave dhow': the cross to Tom M.S. Highflyer.

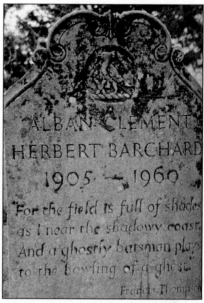

A cricketing theme on the headstone of Alban Barchard at Boxgrove.

other men proudly advertise on their headstones.

The same applies to the Barchard epitaph, which borrows lines from 'At Lords' by the 'Hound of Heaven' poet Francis Thompson, who lived at Storrington:

For the field is full of shades
as I near the shadowy coast,
And a ghostly batsman plays
to the bowling of a ghost.

An altogether more heroic pursuit was followed by Henry Tracy Coxwell (died 1900) who owned an aeronautics factory in Seaford but was better known as an enthusiastic balloonist – or, to those who couldn't take his flights seriously, 'balloonatic'. The plaque erected by his widow in East Blatchington church – the *e* in the middle name is a mason's unhappy mistake – tells us that 'of the many remarkable balloon ascents made by him for scientific purposes during his long career, the most notable was from Wolverhampton, September 1862'.

We are given rather more detail, couched in a restrained playfulness, on a stone over his grave in Seaford Cemetery:

IN PEACE
BENEATH THIS STONE REPOSES
HENRY TRACY COXWELL
THE GREATEST OF ALL AERONAUTS.
HIS ASCENTS INTO THE HEAVENS
WERE INNUMERABLE: AND ON 5ᵀᴴ
SEPTEMBER 1862 HE ATTAINED
TO THE GREAT HEIGHT OF MORE
THAN SEVEN MILES. THIS IS THE
HIGHEST POINT EVER REACHED BY
MAN. HAVING THUS IN LIFE
APPROACHED MORE NEARLY THAN
MORTAL THE GATES OF THE INFINITE
HE HAS NOW IN DEATH WITH A
TRUE AND STEDFAST FAITH PASSED
THROUGH INTO REST EVERLASTING.

Plaque in East Blatchington church to the 'balloonatic' who almost reached Heaven.

Five miles over Wolverhampton, Coxwell's companion recorded a temperature of 37 degrees below freezing, then complained of blindness and passed out. Coxwell decided to release some of the gas so that they could descend but, his hands numbed with cold, he was unable to grasp the valve string. It was only after they had riisen to a height of more than seven miles that he managed to grab the string in his teeth and tug it.

Calendarial oddities

A memorial in the church at Horsted Keynes records the death of Henry Pigott:

Born Decem' ye 30ᵀᴴ 1715
Buried March 7ᵀᴴ 1715.

This only *seems* to be the nonsensical tale of a lad who died several months before he was born, the explanation being that it wasn't until 1751 that England fell into line with the rest of Europe over the New Style calendar. Until that time the new year began on March 25 – so little Henry was buried when he was just over two months old.

The Roman Catholic countries on the continent had adjusted their calendars back in 1582, on the instructions of Pope

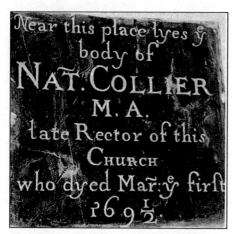

This year, next year . . . Nathaniel Collier's memorial at Jevington gives us a choice of the year in which he died.

Gregory XIII, and by the time that we followed suit (changing the beginning of the year to January 1 at the same time), the authorities decided that September 2 1752 should be followed by September 14 in order to iron out the accumulated errors of centuries. There were disturbances throughout the land that September ('Give us back our eleven days!' was the cry), but many people had long been clamouring for the change to be made. A memorial in Jevington church seems strangely undecided:

Near this place lyes ye
body of
NAT. COLLIER
M.A.
late Rector of this
CHURCH
who dyed Mar:ye first
169½

Collier presumably died on the first day of March 1691 according to the prevailing calendar, but over the water 1692 was already two months old when he died. His

plaque with its queer 91/92 alternatives seems to be having it both ways.

A one-off? No: in Burwash church is a tablet to Elizabeth Casson which gives her date of death as February 14, 1679/80.

A graveslab set into the floor at Laughton church is curious in quite another way:

Here Lyes ye Body
of DINAH, wife of Wᵐ BENGE
Gent. Late of Wadhurst
who Died 7ber 14 1721 Aged
63 Years.

'7ber' for September: there is, I think, no other example of a month appearing in this fashion on a Sussex memorial. Although now the ninth month, September was, as its Latin root (sept) implies, the seventh month of the old Roman year.

Home, sweet home

Jack and Jill windmills on Henry Longhurst's headstone at Keymer.

It's rare to find an engraving of the deceased's home on a tombstone, but it has to be admitted that the golfing writer and broadcaster Henry Longhurst had an exceptional address. He lived in Jack, the black tower mill which stands alongside Jill, a white smock mill, on the Downs above Clayton – and above his last resting place in Keymer churchyard, too. The two famous windmills grace the top of his stone.

S/he was . . .what?

A much-quoted epitaph from Petworth employs a strange rhetorical device:

> She was! She was! She was, what?
> She was all that a woman should be,
>   she was that.

The writer is, as it were, caught in the act of trying to do justice to the dead woman, finally coming up with a complimentary statement which does, however, rely on an exceedingly dull rhyme.

Unique, surely? But no: there are other examples in strikingly similar vein across the country. Samuel Whittby's plaque in the chancel at West Chiltington, for instance, tells us that he died on January 12, 1816, at the age of 59, and continues:

> "He was —
> "But words are wanting to say what,
> "Think what a husband,Father,Friend,should be;
>   And he was that."

Note the mason's desperate attempt (the words cramped and squashed close together) to contain that long third line.

Wrong side of the blanket

Admissions of illegitimacy are rare on gravestones, and understandably so, but no other interpretation of the following epitaph at Cowfold seems possible. A study of the wording (was A.E. a cousin of the captain?) suggests a complex family tangle:

> In fondest memory of
> ALLESINA AVIS MARY ALISON-ALSTON
> Blood daughter of CAPT. G.A. COLES RN
> D.S.O. & MRS A. A. ALISON-ALSTON sister of
> A.E. COLES
> Born JANUARY 21st 1919
> Died 9th JANUARY 1979.

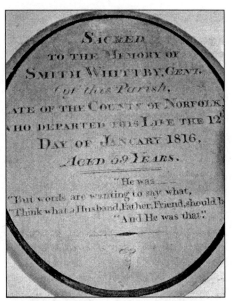

A strange rhetorical device on a memorial at West Chiltington.

Bodily pure

There seems, on the other hand, not to have been the slightest whisper about Margaret Johnson of Chailey. Virginity is perhaps less highly prized today than once it was, and is surely statistically rarer, but her memoirist clearly counted it a virtue:

> Here lyeth the body
> of MARGARET JOHNSON
> who lived ninety
> and two years and
> died a maid the
> 12th day of March
> 1707.

Nothing good enough

Mental anguish is far less frequently recorded than physical, but a Friston epitaph suggests a lifetime of exhausted striving:

> HAUNTED BY PERFECTION

Benefactors

Wooden boards detailing the former generosity of local men and women are common in our churches, and many of their charities still pay small sums to the poor of the parish. None, surely, has such an amazingly long-running 'dole' ceremony as the one founded by Nicholas 'Beggarman' Smith.

A wealthy man, who had (or so the story goes) travelled far and wide through Sussex disguised as a beggar in search of a genuinely friendly place in which to see out his days, Smith finally found a warm welcome in Hartfield, where he settled down. In his will of October 18, 1634, he left money to be shared by forty poor parishioners in perpetuity – and, all these centuries later, the rector still stands by his tomb each Good Friday morning ready to dispense charity to those prepared to ask for it.

In the church at Yapton is a tablet to Stephen Roe who, in his will of 1766, 'gave the Interest on Twelve Hundred Pounds (Three per cent. South Sea Annuities) to the Poor of this Parish yearly for ever.' This charity, too, is still functioning, with half the annual payout going to seven old parishioners and the rest to the church school, though it's doubtful that the recipients' gratitude can do justice to the fulsome verse on Roe's memorial:

The Parent hence shall ne'er depart,
But lead each Babe with joyful heart,
To view this Sacred Stone.
Here gratitude delights to dwell,
And Young and Old shall always tell,
The good that Roe has done.
Soft pity now shall comfort woe,
And ign'rance learn herself to know,
By bounty taught and fed.
Orphans and Widows more and more,
And children yet unborn shall pour
Their blessings on him dead.

There we were, waiting at the church: rector Paddy Craig and churchwarden Kate Allen stand by 'Beggarman' Smith's tomb at Hartfield on Good Friday morning 1997, waiting in vain for someone to ask for charity. For the second year in succession, nobody arrived. The last recipient had been Bessy Hooker, a widow, in 1995.

He damned a king . . .

John Cawley, a wealthy brewer who was three times mayor of Chichester and who died in 1621, has a fine, painted memorial in the cathedral, but its original inscription was later replaced so that it might include the story of his son, William:

IN 1647 HE REPRESENTED THIS CITY IN PARLIAMENT AND IN THE DISPUTES WHICH AROSE IN THE REIGN OF KING CHARLES, HE WAS ONE OF THOSE WHO SIGNED THE DEATH WARRANT OF THAT UNFORTUNATE MONARCH. UPON THE RESTORATION HE WAS EXCEPTED OUT OF THE ACT OF OBLIVION.

Cawley, that is, was not one of the majority forgiven for their actions during the Commonwealth. He fled to the continent when Charles II came to the throne, dying in Bruges six years later.

The man who saved King Charles: Nicholas Tettersell's tomb at St Nicholas, Brighton.

. . . and he saved one

Captain Nicholas Tettersell (the spelling of his surname seems to have been infinitely variable) was a benefactor of a kind: he sailed the future Charles II across the Channel to safety in the early hours of October 15, 1651, his royal passenger having been on the run since the Battle of Worcester. He thought himself insufficiently rewarded after the Restoration in 1660 – as his epitaph in St Nicholas's churchyard, Brighton, makes clear. The last couplet pays affectionate tribute to his wife:

Captain Nicholas Tattersal, through whose prudence, valour and loyalty, Charles II, King of England, after he had escaped the sword of his merciless rebels, and his forces received a fatal overthrow at Worcester, September the 3rd, 1651, was faithfully preserved and conveyed to France, departed this life the 26th of July 1674.

*Within this marble monument doth lie
Approved faith, honour, and loyalty;
In this cold clay he has now ta'en up his
                                    station,
Who once preserv'd the Church, the
                        Crown and Nation:
When Charles ye Greate was nothing
                              but a breath
This valiant soule stept between him and
                                      death:
Usurpers' threats, nor tyrant rebels' frown
Could not affright his duty to the Crown:
Which glorious act of his for Church and
                                      State
Three Princes in one day did gratulate,
Professing all to him in debts to be
As all the world are to his memory.
Since earth could not reward the worth
                                him given,
He now receives it from the King of Heaven.
In the same chest one Jewel more you have,
The partner of his virtues, bed and grave.*

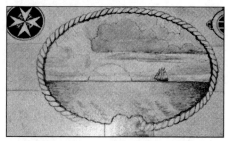

Lady Brassey's memorial at Catsfield gives the exact location of her burial at sea.

Latitude and longitude

Several Sussex memorials record the sad fact of a death overseas, but Lady Brassey's at Catsfield is unusual in two respects: she was buried at sea, and her epitaph gives the precise location :

SACRED TO THE MEMORY OF
ANNIE LADY BRASSEY
DIED AT SEA 14 SEPTEMBER 1887
COMMITTED TO THE DEEP AT
SUNSET IN LAT. 15° 50' S, LONG. 110° 35' E

Born Annie Allnutt, the daughter of a wealthy wine merchant and jockey, she married Thomas Brassey, who inherited the fortune and title of his famous railway contractor father. Their home was the mock-Gothic Normanhurst Court in Catsfield, but the couple spent much of their time abroad on their steam yacht *Sunbeam*. She contracted malaria when with her husband on board the yacht, dying on September 17, 1887 while they were between Australia and Mauritius.

Not so famous last words

A grand wall monument of 1628 in Cuckfield church stresses the piety of 27-year-old Ninian Burrell by giving us the words he is supposed to have spoken on his deathbed. This was a very expensive marble affair, so the strange spellings and inconsistencies were presumably regarded as legitimate at the time. Note, should you visit the church for a close inspection, not only the unusual *XXIIX* (rather than *XXVIII*) for 28, but the equally strange carving of *MD*: it seems that this otherwise competent mason lost his nerve when it came to carving an ornate *M*, medieval fashion, and that he likewise funked joining the vertical stroke and the half-circle of the *D*:

HE WAS A STUDENT OF GOOD
LEARNING AT OXFORD; WHERE HE
LIVED THREE YEARES FELLOW
COMMONER OF WADDAM COLLEDG:
AFTERWARD HE GAVE HIMSELFE TO YE
STUDIE OF YE LAW AT LONDON; WHERE
HE LIVED FOR THE SPACE OF FIVE
YEARES IN YE MIDDLE TEMPLE: AND
BEING XXVII YEARES OLD, DIED OF A
CONSUMPTION AT LONDON; YE X: DAY
OF NOVEMBER IN YE YEARE OF CHRIST
MDC.XXIIX: AND HERE BEING BURIED
WAITETH FOR YE SECOND COMING OF
YE MESSIAH.

His words as he laye on his death bed

MY FLESH & MY HART FAILETH, BUT
GOD IS YE STRENGTH OF MY HART &
MY PORTION FOR EVER.

'Damaris': she died of a broken heart.

Him, him and her

Although we are accustomed to seeing, atop ancient marble tombs, the great lord with his two wives on either side, the reverse takes us by surprise. An epitaph at Worth:

SACRED
TO THE MEMORY OF
DAVID GORING
DIED FEB. 10 1830
AGED 39 YEARS
Also of
JONATHAN COLLINS
DIED OCT 9 1875
AGED 72 YEARS
And of
BARBARA
THEIR WIFE
DIED OCT 4 1878
AGED 85 YEARS.

A love story

By the west wall of the churchyard at Brede stands a wooden cross *(facing page)* with only one word on it:

Damaris

Here lies Damaris Richardson, a beautiful orphan girl who, living in the village with her uncle, fell in love with wealthy young Lewis Smith from Church House. Although they became engaged, his parents forbade the marriage on the grounds of their social inequality.

Poor Damaris died of a broken heart at the age of 22 and was buried on September 4, 1856, at the spot where the lovers used to meet.

As for Lewis, his sweetheart's memory seems to have been sufficient for him: he died a bachelor at Church House forty years later.

A sheep breeder

John Ellman of Glynde (1753-1832) was the man responsible, almost single-handedly, for developing the Southdown breed of sheep, improving both the quality of its wool and the quantity of its hindquarter mutton. Nationally famous though he became, he rejected a title and was a model employer, housing his unmarried workers under his own roof and sharing his meal table with them, too.

When he retired, nearly two hundred noblemen and farmers from all over the country presented him with a massive silver tureen surmounted by the model of a Southdown sheep. He has a large tomb in the churchyard at Glynde.

The chunky Southdown is now, alas, a rare breed:

BY HIM THE BREED OF SOUTH DOWN SHEEP WAS FIRST IMPROVED AND THRO HIS EXERTIONS SPREAD OVER THE WHOLE KINGDOM. A GREAT PORTION OF HIS LIFE WAS SPENT IN RENDERING PRACTICAL ASSISTANCE TO PUBLIC IMPROVEMENTS; AT THE SAME TIME HE DID NOT FORGET TO PROMOTE THE WELFARE AND HAPPINESS OF THE INHABITANTS OF THIS PARISH IN WHICH HE RESIDED FOR MORE THAN 60 YEARS.

He bred the Southdown: John Ellman's tomb at Glynde.

A horsewoman

Betty Clark was a keen horsewoman who died in 1947 at the tragically young age of 23. Her headstone in the churchyard at Westmeston has the head of her horse Toby on it, next to an epitaph which not

only takes a positive view of death, but manages to suggest something of her personality, too:

SHE HAS COME TO THE LAST OF THE GATEWAYS, HAS LAUGHED AND GONE GALLOPING THROUGH.

Mayday

Many things we take for granted have required a stroke of the imagination. By the church door at Selmeston is a small headstone dated March 1, 1962:

*IN MEMORY OF
OUR BELOVED
STANLEY
MOCKFORD
AGED 64
AIR RADIO PIONEER
AND ORIGINATOR OF
THE DISTRESS CALL
MAYDAY*

Yours faithfully

Even simple words can change their meaning over the centuries, and the adjective chosen for Henry Rogers on a brass floor slab at Selmeston meant – as we learn from the dialect dictionary compiled by a later vicar of the same church, William Parish – only that he was a painstaking character:

*THE BODY OF HENRY ROGERS
A PAINEFULL PREACHER IN THIS CHURCH
TWO
AND THIRTY YEERES WHO DYED THE SIXT
OF
MAY ANO DNI 1639 AND IN THE YEERE
OF HIS AGE 67 LYETH HEERE EXPECTING
THE SECOND COMING OF OUR LORD
JESUS CHRIST
I DID BELEEVE AND THEREFORE SPAKE
WHEREOF I TAUGH I DOE PERTAKE*
Henry Rogers

There are, in fact, several epitaphs to painful preachers (at Petworth, Ringmer and Southease, for instance). The most striking feature of the Rogers inscription is the apparent signature of Henry Rogers himself at the foot of the epitaph. Since it's difficult to be believe (though pleasant to

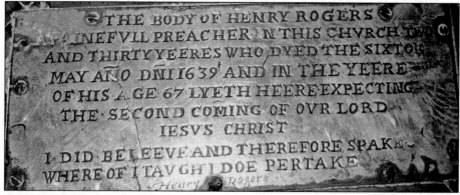

Brass, with apparent signature, in memory of a 'painefull' preacher at Selmeston.

imagine) that he scratched it while on his deathbed, perhaps the freehand style was intended to emphasise the fact that the last two lines (with their mason's mistake) were in his own voice.

Heartbreakers

There is surely no Sussex epitaph more touching than the lines written for Martha Feist on a table tomb in the churchyard at Cuckfield. She died on September 26, 1818, at the age of 25, leaving not only her husband but her little ones behind:

> *Oh husband dear my time is past*
> *You remain while life doth last*
> *And now for me no sorrow take*
> *But love my children for my sake.*

A tombstone of 1792 at Edburton remembers (with another mason's mistake) Sarah Strevens:

> *A loving Wife, a Parent kind*
> *Six children dear she left behind;*
> *Repent in time make no delay*
> *For in my prime was took away*

An ancient stone at Worth, the last lines lost, marks the grave of a child:

> *My*
> *mother dear greav*
> *no more for your child*
> *the time I stay'd with*
> *you was but a little wile*

And at Petworth, on a stone to Henry and Jane Nash, who died in infancy:

> *Scarce had we seen ye sun & liv'd but death*
> *Obscur'd its rays & took away our breath.*

Finding the right words for such a loss must be an agony. Isaac Murrell of Barnham was only 14 months old when he

Striking headstone for a child's grave at Wivelsfield.

died: he is described, movingly, as 'This little lamb that was so small.'

Ernest Udny, who died in 1808 at the age of seven, was (according to the memorial raised by his grandmother in Chichester Cathedral) 'an amiable and most endearing Child'. This rather lukewarm remembrance is offset by a moving quatrain:

> *E're Sin cou'd blight or Sorrow fade*
> *Death came with friendly Care*
> *The op'ning Bud to Heav'n convey'd*
> *And bade it blossom there.*

It is, of course, impossible to ponder any child's epitaph without a feeling of deep sadness, but some modern headstones are given a special tenderness by the illustration of favourite animals. At Wivelsfield eleven-year-old Amy Turner's memorial is actually given the shape of her cat. The wording is affectingly simple:

> *Our beloved daughter*
> *sister and friend*
> *who smiled her way*
> *through life.*

Christianos!

Since Henry Rochester died (on May 28, 1646) as soon as he had been christened, we must assume that he was but a baby. His memorial on the vestry floor at Selmeston nevertheless speaks in world-weary tones. The verse (like the spelling) is rough-hewn, but it has a colloquial vigour and a splendid ruggedness. It is preceded by an 'apostrophe' – a call for attention to all who pass by:

APOSTROPHE AD
OMNES

THIS LIFE THATS PACKT WTH JELOSIES & FEARS
I LOVE NOT THAT'S BEYOND YE LISTS OF TEARS
THAT LIFE FOR ME. FOE HERE I CANNOT BREATH
MY PRAYERS OUT. THERE I SHALL HAVE WREATH
TO SAY OUR FATHER THATS IN HEAVEN WTH ME
WHERE CHORES OF SANCTS & INNOCENTS
THERE BE
CHRISTIANOS

NO SOONER CHRISTENED BUT POSSESSION
I TOOK OF TH HEAVENLIE HABITATION

That *foe* in the third line should be *for*, and the *wreath* at the end of the fourth line would surely make more sense as *breath*, but more striking is the 90-degree angle between the verse and Henry's name and date of death.

The probable explanation is that this part was inscribed first, so that the stone coud be positioned in the churchyard awaiting permission for a prized site within the church itself. Once that was granted, the memorial could be lifted from the ground, the verse being inscribed on the alignment that its length demanded.

The unborn

Aficionados of horror are accustomed to the idea of the 'undead', but the opposite notion is to be found on a memorial stone set into the vestry floor at Berwick. This is to Rev. George Hall, whose 'name speaks all learning Humane and Divine'. His epitaph ends with words suggesting that his life has been put sharply into reverse:

unborn january the 15th 1668

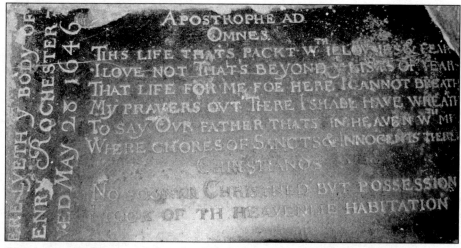

'Here I cannot breath my prayers out . . .' Memorial to Henry Rochester at Selmeston.

Weald and Downs

Most notable writers on Sussex have come from outside, but two home-grown talents are remembered in appropriate places.

Arthur Beckett, founder/editor of *The Sussex County Magazine*, is buried at Friston with his wife Alice, and their epitaph tells us that *THEY LOVED THESE DOWNS*. What better decoration for their headstone than that 'the pride of Sussex', the round-headed rampion?

Wilfred Scawen Blunt – poet, Arabist, amateur diplomat, horse-breeder and amorist – is buried in the grounds of his home near Southwater, Newbuildings Place, and lines from his poem *Chanclebury Ring* are inscribed on his tombstone:

Dear checker-work of woods, the Sussex Weald.
If a name thrills me yet of things on earth,
That name is thine! How often I have fled
To thy deep hedgerows and embraced
each field,
Each lag, each pasture - fields which gave
me birth
And saw my youth, and which must hold
me dead.

The sailors' friend

The rocks at the foot of Beachy Head are treacherous for mariners, and Parson Jonathan Darby, rector of East Dean from 1705, saved dozens of lives by digging out a series of caves and tunnels in the chalk cliff at Beachy Head, in which he fastened lanterns to warn of the danger. He died on October 26, 1726, and his headstone pays tribute to his kindness:

HE WAS THE SAILORS' FRIEND.

Round-head rampions on the gravestone of writer Arthur Beckett at Friston.

While on her travels

Young Emmerline Champneys Garner of Grantham, in the Midlands, was evidently wont to think on death. Her floorslab tells us that:

While living she desired to be buried
wherever life departed.

In the event it departed on October 29, 1807, when she was only eighteen, and her wish wasn't fulfilled to the very letter Emmerline died in Tunbridge Wells but is buried at Frant.

An inventor

Readers with good memories may recall the name of Edmund Cartwright (1743–1823) from school history lessons. The inventor of the power loom has a large plaque in the church at Battle. He was, apparently, also a poet, although the example given on his memorial suggests that, though competent enough, he was wise to stick to the day job:

When Death shall approach with his terrors,
Resigned may I bend to the rod;
And, tho' loaded with crimes and with errors,
Repose on the mercies of God.

Ancient & Modern

Thomas and Emma Attewell have an unusual grave at Cuckfield. Their names are carved into the kerb, and are a little hard to spot, while pride of place is given to No. 140 from 'Hymns Ancient & Modern', complete with musical staves: *Jesus Lives!*

No. 140 in your hymn book: an unusual musical flourish on a grave at Cuckfield.

A prince of Denmark

A Danish soldier who became an anchorite is remembered at St John sub Castro church, Lewes. Prince Magnus ('Mangnus' in the inscription) had himself walled up in the original church here, and his exploits were recorded on an arch leading into the chancel. When the old church was replaced in 1839, this was set

Prince Magnus was a Danish nobleman who had himself walled up at St John sub Castro, Lewes, as an anchorite.

into the outside wall. Parts have evidently been recarved (the earliest lettering is in a medieval Lombardic script). Magnus, we learn, 'becoming disgusted with the world and all earthly things, the vanity and vexation of which his own unhappy experience had taught him, retired from society and became an anchorite'.

Just awful

Many an epitaph understandably makes the best of a bad job, but there's no reason why we should all go quietly. A stone at Udimore:

> IN MEMORY OF
> John WOODHAMS
> Senr whose awful
> change was on July
> the 23^d 1776 after
> a life of 66
> years

Good sorts

Since most epitaphs are anodyne affairs, it's pleasant to come across those which, without being in any way eccentric, yet manage to give the dead a sense of his or her individuality.

At Westmeston, for instance, Albert Coomber, who died in 1970 at the age of 67, is remembered as 'one of nature's gentlemen'.

There are two in similar vein at Isfield. Iain Buchanan (died 1973) is given the heart-warming epithet 'a truly honest man', while a stone close by salutes Thomas Buckeridge (died 1987), 'who was never dull'.

Let there be more like them!

Puns upon a time

There was, as Nicholas Pelham's memorial reveals *(page 13)* a taste for punning epitaphs in days gone by. If the practice seems a touch flippant, we should remember that it had a respectable precedent in heraldry. Amon and Amon Henry Wilds, the father and son team responsible (with Charles Busby) for much of Brighton's Regency architecture, were following in a long tradition when they devised the ammonite 'logo' reproduced in huge form on Amon's tomb in the churchyard of St Nicholas, Brighton.

An ammonite was the punning trademark of Amon Wilds, Brighton's Regency builder and architect, who died in 1833.

At Brightling, a Latin inscription in the chancel to the infant son of Thomas Pye, rector from 1590, plays on the family name. A translation reads:

The Lord gave, the Lord hath taken away.
Pious live, Pious die

On the north wall of the Lady Chapel at Ringmer is an obscure verse:

For all heaven's gifts (in many single set)
In Jefferays – mayney altogether met.

To make sense of this hard-working conceit you need to know that the memorial (an alabaster monument with two kneeling figures) honours 'Mrs Elizabeth Jefferay, wife of Walter Mayney'.

Pompous, moi?

There's another visual pun in St Anne's church, Lewes, where the brass to Dr Thomas Twyne shows two serpents – entwined. The Twyne memorial offers us a prime example of praise become ridiculous by its very excess. The church guide gives a translation from the Latin:

Alas, he is dead, our Doctor! Here he lies, and lightly on him lies the earth. When he passed away, Sussex sank down faint and nigh to death; and Disease grew strong, rejoiced to behold his great adversary quelled. But when Hippocrates, the Master of all Healers, saw the corpse, surely, he mused, this sacred dust transmuted should be a remedy to disease, and ashes prevail against ashes.

As for Sir Nicholas Parker, it seems that his like should never be expected again. Born in 1604, he adopted the Roundhead cause during the Civil War and served for a time as Cromwell's secretary. The inscription on his tomb in Willingdon churchyard goes right over the top:

Then blame not aged Britain's feeble womb
For in her Parker's birth she did consume
Her utmost strength. The world will scarce
*   be strong*
For such another brave conception.

In fairness, we should make the point that most such epitaphs were devised not by the deceased themselves (who should therefore be accounted blameless), but by their earnest friends and families.

Maids in a field

The village sign at Mayfield suggests pictorially, though unconvincingly, that the place gets its name from maids playing in a field. It's no doubt nothing but a curious coincidence, but a fine carving on one of the headstones in the churchyard depicts what could be just such a scene. The wording is badly worn, but the date is something like 1799 (only the last digit is debatable) and this is almost certainly the grave of John Soper's wife: her name is not decipherable, but his stone stands next to hers.

Although this could, indeed, be a scene of innocent play, it is perhaps not fanciful to read the picture in quite another way. Soper died a few years later in his sixties, which suggests that his wife was unlikely to be known for playing childish games in what appears to be an orchard. And our knowledge of the Cook and Rusbridger headstones at Walberton in the west of the county *(page 22)* alerts us to the possibility that this is, in fact, a death scene. Has the woman on the left been thrown from the

A mysterious gravestone at Mayfield. Does the carving depict an accidental death?

horse (which, granted, has a somewhat docile look) or has she, perhaps, fallen from the tree while, say, picking apples?

Nicknames

Churchyard rules demanding a seemly restraint certainly don't apply in the Brighton and Preston Cemetery, which is part of the Lewes Road complex at Brighton. Those who despise polished marble, heart-shaped stones, colour photographs of the deceased and dire verses apparently culled from the obituary columns of local newspapers will find much to incense them here.

Hunters of the unusual, on the other hand, will surely enjoy the unfettered expressions of grief and, especially, the array of affectionate nicknames. Mum, dad and gramps are everywhere, but find themselves upstaged by such as:

OUR DEAREST "MUMBLES",
BELOVED WIFE OF HENRY, "DIDS"

not to speak of treasures such as:

GEORGE (MONKEY)
NEWINGTON

and

GEORGE E. LANGFORD,
"WEASEL".

Someone should make a list of the (once) cheerful crew congregating the area around the cemetery chapel. Their number includes *Winty, Schoo* and *Our Tut* – and the graveyard would be a poorer place without them.

The cruellest month

Readers who know the works of John Donne and the metaphysical poets will enjoy two sets of verse typical of the period on the Glyd monument inside Brightling church. Richard Glyd died on Easter Day, April 5, 1618:

His neighbours breasts will common place
bookes make
Writt full of's prayse: who's next for Index take.
Their successors of th'unborn age will crye
Taught by tradition's fayth here Glyd doth lye.
Prove friends unkind this marble stone shall
weepe,
And time in sheding tears with Aprill keepe.

Glyd's wife Martha died on April 24 the following year, and the poet, having made play with the idea of seasonal showers in his first verse, finds it a fitting coincidence that both should die in the same month:

Rest blameless soule: friends, neighbours all
bidd sleepe.
Thou hast noe foes waking thy ghost to keepe.
Sleepe neare thy mate: Aprill you both intombs.
Why should one flesh, one hart take up two
rooms.

Protestant martyrs

There are several memorials in Sussex to the Protestant victims of Bloody Queen Mary, all of them raised centuries after their violent deaths. At East Grinstead there's a churchyard monument to martyrs who were burned in the High Street during the summer of 1556, while a stone outside Colkins Mill church in Mayfield honours local Protestants who were put to death in the same year. The first of the Sussex martyrs (burned at Lewes on July 15, 1555) was the Flemish brewer Derrick

Monument to seventeen Protestant martyrs on Cliffe Hill, Lewes.

Carver, and there's a plaque to him in Black Lion Lane, Brighton. At Warbleton, set into the church wall, is a memorial to another who died at Lewes, the ironmaster Richard Woodman. Best known of all is the obelisk on Cliffe Hill, above Lewes, which was erected in 1901:

IN LOVING MEMORY
OF THE UNDERNAMED
SEVENTEEN PROTESTANT
MARTYRS,
WHO FOR THEIR FAITHFUL
TESTIMONY TO
GOD'S TRUTH,
WERE, DURING THE REIGN OF
QUEEN MARY,
BURNED TO DEATH
IN FRONT OF THE THEN STAR
INN – NOW THE TOWN HALL –
LEWES.

Parish servants

We end our miscellany in the most fitting way, with two faithful servants of the church at Worth.

Isaac Tullett of Worth Park died in 1897 at the age of 70, and the massive bell on his headstone is the clue to the sterling service he gave. Fine lettering down one side reads *a bellringer at this church*. The matching script on the other side is too badly worn to read, but presumably recorded the number of years he pulled on the ropes.

A bellringer's headstone at Worth.

But it is John Alcorn who deservedly gets the last word. Not only is the verse on his headstone among the most skilful to be found anywhere in Sussex, but the man himself was an enthusiast of the churchyard. He died in 1868 at the age of 81, having been parish clerk at Worth for many years.

The composer of his epitaph (Charles Curle, a relative of the rector) described him as 'one of the last of the church clerks, perhaps the very last, for the present kind-hearted incumbent allowed him to continue in office long after a clerk's part in the services had fallen everywhere else into disuse. Old John was a hardy, cheery old man, and took great delight in digging graves':

Time-honoured friend! for fifty-three full years
He saw each bridal's joy, each burial's tears:
Within the walls by Saxons reared of old:
By the stone sculptured font of antique mould,
Under the massive arches in the glow
Tinged by dyed sun-beams, passing to and fro,
A sentient portion of the sacred place,
A worthy presence with a well-worn face.

The lich-gate's shadow o'er his pall at last
Bids kind adieu as poor old John goes past:
Unseen the path, the trees, the old oak door;
Nor more his footfalls touch the tomb-paved
                                          floor:
His silvery head is hid, his service done,
Of all those sabbaths absent only one.
And now amid the graves he delved around,
He rests and sleeps beneath the hallowed
                                          ground.

A MODERN MASTER

Ours is an age of cremations and 'green' burials, of small plaques, memorial benches and trees planted in quiet retreats. It is, too, an age of graveyard best behaviour, when the stubborn few who persist in raising headstones to their dead quickly discover that our stern finger-wagging watchdogs of respectability have firm rules about the materials that may be used and the words (no 'mum' or 'gran' say some) that may be inscribed upon them – a restriction which, if enforced in ages past, would have denied us many of the riches celebrated in these pages.

While it should follow that any modern burial ground will be uniformly dull and

John Skelton at work in his studio at Streat.

uninspiring, however, the good news is that the descendants of those skilful eighteenth century masons are still working among us. Only a small minority of us will seek these craftsmen out, rather than leave so apparently routine a matter to the undertaker, but in churchyards across Sussex the visitor will stumble upon memorials whose very quality proclaims that they have been individually commissioned, designed and executed.

Pre-eminent among our lettercutters is the sculptor John Skelton who, in 1940, as a young man of seventeen, was apprenticed to his famous uncle Eric Gill. His work is internationally known but, in common with the hundred or so kindred spirits now at work throughout England, he makes no artistic distinction between the grand commission and the humble: enter his workshop in Streat, near Ditchling, and you are as likely to find him carving a memorial for an ordinary local family as (to take one example among many) for the writer George Eliot in Westminster Abbey.

In this chapter, with illustrations from his own portfolio, John Skelton recalls his early days as a lettercutter; offers a fascinating insider's view of the art; and gives us his opinion of its state of health today:

❛ Eric Gill didn't actually stand over you, but he had his own workshop close by and he'd come across half way through the morning and again in the afternoon. He could be critical about some of the things you did, and I well remember knocking a corner off the stone while doing my first bit of lettercutting for him. Although in a sense the job was a test piece, it had a real purpose and a site: it was to be a 'tile' in Gill's kitchen floor, showing the orientation,

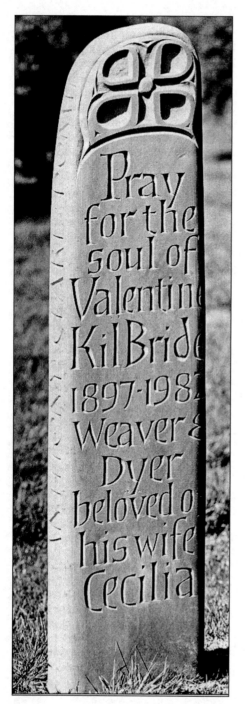

magnetic variation and date. I apologised for my carelessness and suggested that I could get over it by breaking off the other corner to match. He was very put out. He wasn't exactly furious, but he said: 'No. You've made a mistake: don't try and cover it up.' So I had to put the moulding along the stone and round the broken corner. I still have a rubbing of it in my workshop as a reminder. **'**

Masons' mistakes

' I do sympathise with masons whose errors are forever written in stone. It's possible to resurface the stone by rubbing down the offending letter and blending out the rubbing so that it doesn't show – except to a keen eye in the setting sun or the early dawn – but it's quite a job. I've had to do it two or three times, but only the first time was it my own fault.

It was just after the war, and I was employed by an old fashioned firm. I was working on a piece of Yorkshire stone, and I misread an *F* for an *E*. I was just out of the army and anxious to make my living, so I got up in the morning before the other men got to work and rubbed down this stone in my own time until I'd removed the bottom bar. Then I recut the letter and the letters around it, and it took me a lot of early mornings and late evenings to do it.

The boss came round after I'd finished, and he said: 'Well, John, you've saved time.' He could see that I didn't understand what he was driving at. 'Ah,' he said. 'You've saved time in your future life, because you'll never do that again!' And he was right. It's surprising how your mind can wander, and the trick is to read the inscription backwards, letter by letter. **'**

Headstone for a weaver and dyer in Ditchling churchyard. John Skelton/red sandstone.

Materials

❛ None of our Sussex stones is really good enough for memorials. Sussex marble is full of crustaceans. It's a quirky material, really – you can't cut letters in it. And Sussex sandstone is too soft. I know that it *has* been used for headstones, and I've come across some even up to two hundred years old with the original inscriptions still legible, but that's highly unusual.

By and large we use fairly traditional materials such as Portland and York stone. There's also Hoptonwood stone from Derbyshire, a limestone known as English marble. Slate is one of the things I specialise in. It will take beautiful lettering and delicate carving, too, but it's a very critical medium – every scratch shows. The important thing is to select the material to suit the job. ❜

This playful headstone at Streat has a fossilised sea urchin (or shepherd's purse) from the Sussex chalk in the centre of the word 'geologist'. John Skelton/Purbeck Portland.

Churchyard rules

❛ The church authorities produce a list of what is acceptable. They don't encourage marble or granite, but they do occasionally get through: the vicar may allow it. I know that some people find this awfully interfering, but I have to say that I'm in general agreement with the policy.

A marble headstone so obviously isn't an English thing. The material started coming here during the Victorian period, when ease of transport made it feasible, but it's quite out of keeping with a Sussex country churchyard. Black marble usually has to be polished to a very high degree.

All stones change colour naturally with time, but marbles weather an unsightly green. In fact, all stones will go green if they're near trees, which they usually are: they need regular cleaning.

As for granite, it does last virtually for ever, but it's so hard that in my view it's not possible to cut really decent letters in it, unless they're huge – for the base of a monument or a statue, perhaps. It's true that some black Swedish granites are very fine but, again, they really don't suit a Sussex churchyard.

Vicars can be very choosy about what you're allowed to put on the stone, but I've never had any trouble on that score. ❜

A child's headstone at Chailey, illustrating the plants and animals that she loved. John Skelton/slate.

Memorial plaques by John Skelton at Boxgrove (*left*, Hoptonwood stone) and West Dean, West Sussex (slate).

Meeting the client

❝ I like to think that I follow in a long line of village masons commissioned to produce a memorial headstone on the instructions of a member of the family. That said, people often don't know what they want to say, so I tend to suggest that they come back with an inscription and I'll advise them whether it's suitable.

Quite honestly, the least you say is generally best. A lot of people come up with rather too much, and I have to try to persuade them that it would be more in keeping – and, of course, cheaper – if it were cut down a bit.

I remember being asked to record on a child psychiatrist's headstone that he 'loved all cats and some children'. After some deliberation we came up with the rather less controversial 'lover of cats and children'. And I have refused a job. It was an epitaph for a man responsible for some kind of machine gun 'by which invention two world wars were shortened and many lives saved'. I couldn't go along with that sentiment, I'm afraid. ❞

Costings

❝ It's obvious that a memorial which is individually designed must be more expensive than something which is, in effect, mass-produced, although a funeral director who takes instructions and passes them on to somebody else will want to take his cut.

It really isn't possible to give an average figure, because the choice of stone and design makes every memorial unique, but if you're paying something like a thousand pounds for a funeral you may think it well worth while to pay, say, another seven hundred pounds or so to have a headstone of genuine quality.

Basically I work out the number of letters, their height, intricacy and so on, and charge by the hour. ❞

Modern standards

❝ I was trained, although I of course wasn't a part of it, during an era of mass production. The thirties and the post-war period produced what are known in the trade as 'packing case openers' – in other words, people received memorials ready-made from Italy.

There was a standard memorial which I had to do when I first came out of the army and was employed by somebody else. It had daffodils, lilies and ivy by way of decoration, and you had to carve the same design over and over again. I used to try and hide things in mine, and occasionally my ivy berries would be bosoms, just to liven things up a bit. But nobody knew except me.

The introduction of lead lettering had a very bad effect on standards. What you do is cut the form, drill it with holes and pummel the lead into it. The lead is beaten in cold and then trimmed off with a chisel to give the finish. It's quite a tedious business, and I shouldn't have thought it was very economical, but those who practise it seem to work pretty quickly and it's still done today. Generally, though, the letters aren't well formed.

Another problem, of course, is that they do fall out. The surface of the stone weathers, leaving the lead standing proud, and then water and frost get in behind – not to speak of mischievous choirboys who're after lead pellets for their catapults. That was always the story, anyway, although I was a choirboy and certainly enjoyed firing a catapult, but I never pinched lead letters from headstones.

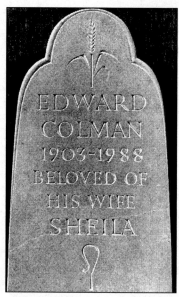

A farmer's headstone at Sompting. John Skelton/Portland stone.

But I do think things are getting better now. In every county there are people who are looking for memorials made by craftsmen, and there are certainly the craftsmen about to make them.

As for my own work, I suppose you can say that everything I do has a Gill touch to it, but I have developed a free style of my own over the years. And of course I adjust the lettering according to the character of the person being commemorated or to the design of the stone: the choice of stone will often dictate the style of the lettering

How can you tell that a memorial is mine? Well, I do usually sign my work, very discreetly. I carve my name and the date up the side of the stone. ❞

GAZETTEER

All sites of memorials listed below are parish churches unless otherwise specified. The first figure refers to the relevant Ordnance Survey Landranger map: seven maps (186-189 and 197-199) cover the whole county. This is followed by the six-figure map reference.

Amberley	197	TQ 028132	Dallington cross	199	TQ 661176
Ardingly	187/198	TQ 339298	Ditchling	198	TQ 326152
Arundel	197	TQ 016074	Dragons Green pub	198	TQ 140235
Ashburnham	199	TQ 689145	Eartham	197	SU 939093
Ashdown Forest			Eastbourne, Old Town	199	TV 598995
'airmen's grave'	188	TQ 458274	Bandstand plaque	199	TV 615985
Battle	199	TQ 750158	Larkin's Field (dog)	199	TV 605988
Berwick	199	TQ 519049	Towner (horse)	199	TV 599994
Bexhill	199	TQ 745081	East Blatchington	198	TV 484998
Billingshurst Chapel	187/197	TQ 086258	East Dean, E. Sussex	199	TV 557977
Bolney	198	TQ 258224	East Dean, W. Sussex	197	SU 905132
Bolney chapel	198	TQ 263235	East Grinstead	187	TQ 397380
Bosham	197	SU 804039	East Lavant	197	SU 863095
Boxgrove	197	SU 908075	Edburton	198	TQ 232115
Brede	199	TQ 825182	Ewhurst Green	199	TQ 796246
Brightling	199	TQ 684210	Felpham	197	SZ 949999
Brighton *(and see Patcham)*			Fletching	198	TQ 429234
Carver plaque	198	TQ 311041	Frant	188	TQ 590357
Lewes Rd cemeteries	198	TQ 328057	Friston	197	TV 552982
Old Jewish cemetery	198	TQ 315065	Glynde	198	TQ 456093
Pets' cemetery	198	TQ 303064	Goring	198	TQ 111027
St Nicholas	198	TQ 307045	Hailsham	199	TQ 592095
Broadwater	198	TQ 146044	Hamsey	198	TQ 414122
Broadwater cemetery	198	TQ 143044	Hartfield	188	TQ 479358
Burpham	197	TQ 039090	Hastings, All Saints	199	TQ 828099
Burton	197	SU 968176	Heathfield *(and see Old Heathfield)*		
Burwash	199	TQ 677248	Gibraltar Tower	199	TQ 588214
Cade Street chapel	199	TQ 614206	Herstmonceux	199	TQ 642102
Catsfield	199	TQ 729134	Highdown, miller	198	TQ 096044
Chailey	198	TQ 392193	Horsham	187	TQ 171303
Chichester Cathedral	197	SU 859048	Horsted Keynes	187/198	TQ 383286
Chiddingly	199	TQ 544142	Hove	198	TQ 287048
Clayton	198	TQ 299139	Hove cemetery	198	TQ 275057
Cocking	197	SU 879175	Hurstpierpoint	198	TQ 279165
Cowfold	198	TQ 213227	St George's	198	TQ 286164
Crawley	187	TQ 268366	Isfield	198	TQ 444182
Crowborough Common			Jevington	199	TQ 561015
Soldiers mem.	188/199	TQ 504293	Keymer	198	TQ 315153
Crowhurst	199	TQ 757123	Kirdford	186/197	TQ 018265
Cuckfield	198	TQ 303245	Laughton	199	TQ 501126

Lewes *(and see S. Malling, Southover)*		
Jireh Chapel	198	TQ 421104
Martyrs memorial	198	TQ 424104
Racecourse (jockey)	198	TQ 394109
St Anne	198	TQ 409100
St John sub Castro	198	TQ 415105
St Michael	198	TQ 413100
Lindfield	198	TQ 349259
Lower Beeding	198	TQ 220275
Mayfield	188/199	TQ 586270
Colkins Mill ch.	188/199	TQ 582269
Newhaven	198	TQ 444012
Ninfield	199	TQ 704123
Northiam	199	TQ 830246
North Stoke	197	TQ 019108
Old Heathfield	199	TQ 599203
Partridge Green		
Hoppit stone	198	TQ 194190
bicycle memorial	198	TQ 184206
Patcham	198	TQ 303092
Chattri	198	TQ 304111
Petworth	197	SU 976219
Playden	189	TQ 920216
Poling	197	TQ 047047
Portslade	198	TQ 259054
Pulborough		
Toat monument	197	TQ 050216
Racton	197	SU 779092
Ringmer	198	TQ 445125
Rottingdean	198	TQ 370026
Rye	189	TQ 922203
Rye Harbour	189	TQ 938203
St Leonards, Silverhill	199	TQ 800108
Seaford	198	TQ 482990
Selmeston	199	TQ 510069
Sidlesham	197	SZ 858974
Singleton	197	SU 878131
Slaugham	187/198	TQ 267281
Slindon	197	SU 961084
Sompting	198	TQ 162056
Southease	198	TQ 422053

Southover	198	TQ 413096
Southwater		
Scawen Blunt grave	198	TQ 141245
South Bersted	197	SU 935002
South Malling	198	TQ 412111
Steyning	198	TQ 177112
Stopham	197	TQ 026189
Streat	198	TQ 351152
Tangmere	197	SU 901062
Thakeham	198	TQ 110174
Tillington	197	SU 964220
Tortington	197	TQ 003050
Trotton	197	SU 836225
Twineham	198	TQ 253200
Uckfield	198	TQ 472215
Udimore	189/199	TQ 863189
Wadhurst	188	TQ 641319
Walberton	197	SU 972057
Warbleton	199	TQ 609183
Warnham	198	TQ 159337
Westbourne	197	SU 755073
Westham	199	TQ 642046
Westmeston	198	TQ 339137
West Burton		
Fred Hughes stone	197	TQ 007137
West Chiltington	197/198	TQ 090183
West Dean, W. Sussex	197	SU 862126
West Grinstead	198	TQ 171207
West Hoathly	187	TQ 363326
West Stoke	197	SU 827087
West Tarring	198	TQ 131041
West Wittering	197	SZ 777985
Willingdon	199	TQ 589025
Butts Brow memorial	199	TQ 579017
Winchelsea	189	TQ 905174
Withyham	188	TQ 494356
Wivelsfield	198	TQ 338208
Worth	198	TQ 302363
Worthing		
'warrior birds'	198	TQ 154027
Yapton	197	SU 982035

Recommended further reading:

Sussex Churches & Chapels by David Beevers, Richard Marks and John Roles (pub. Royal Pavilion, Brighton); *The Buildings of England: Sussex* by Ian Nairn & Nikolaus Pevsner (Penguin); *Collins Guide to Parish Churches* by John Betjeman.

INDEX

DEAD END . . . . .

**a space for you to record
your own chosen epitaph**

What the Vicar Saw

David Arscott

Gloriously indiscreet gleanings
from the Sussex parish registers

for Colin Richards

that old reprobate

*I*magine yourself a Sussex country clergyman a century or two ago. Perhaps you are one of those unhappy third sons of a wealthy family, resigned to life in a rural backwater while your oldest brother swaggers around his inherited estate and the next in line enjoys a high ranking position in the army.

Since it's likely that you are the only man of any education in the neighbourhood, it will hardly be surprising if you spend your solitary free hours pursuing some arcane, academic or antiquarian research in order to fight off boredom and retain your sanity. It's a situation which might have been specifically designed to encourage such obsessions and eccentricities as compiling a dictionary of the Sussex dialect (William Parish at Selmeston); writing more than ten thousand letters to the newspapers (James Bacon-Phillips at Crowhurst); or, the ultimate clerical achievement, breeding a green mouse (Rosslyn Bruce at Herstmonceux).

Now imagine yourself sitting down to make the latest entry in the register of births, deaths and marriages. How tempting, since you take a rather lofty view of your parishioners, to indulge your humour or your waspishness by recording details which emphasise the rich comedy of their lives! You scribble a few words encapsulating their human frailties and sit back contentedly, a little smile upon your lips.

A sense of superiority is but one explanation of these marginal indulgences, however, for our Sussex parsons were not always a cut above their parishioners. The strict keeping of registers was first established in 1540 by Henry VIII, and to read them is to realise that standards of clerical education varied a good deal in the centuries that followed: sometimes we find a flawless Latin being used, sometimes a crude and illiterate English. What remained constant – what must have given a good many vicars the confidence to record their personal opinions and observations – was the fact that, during their own lifetime at least, nobody but their parish clerk would ever get to see them. Secrecy bestowed a delicious licence.

The accuracy and justice of individual remarks is, of course, impossible to verify so many years later. When I was researching this book, one gentleman objected that it might contain material embarrassing for families whose distant relatives featured in it. While it seems improbable that the discovery of a 'base born' or drunken ancestor will cause a reader much discomfiture today (the very opposite, perhaps), it had better be added that what the vicar saw may now and then have been glimpsed through clouded spectacles. This record of past lives in Sussex should not be regarded as any less fallible than the men who, collectively, wrote it.

God bless them, all the same, for their gossipy indiscretions.

David Arscott

Contents

'The day of our death is better than the day of our birth.'

– written on the cover of the Ewhurst parish register

Fond of a Tipple

Rotherfield, 1780
Buried John Basting, otherwise Gin & Bitters.

Many a clergyman must have privately solaced himself with a regular glass or two of port, but the sins of his parishioners were sometimes more glaring.

If John Basting's nickname suggests that he must have been prodigiously fond of the hard stuff, others unhappily took too much and succumbed to it.

Heathfield, 1735
Buried Henry George, a traveller, killed by drinking brandy.

Ticehurst, 1797
This person died at Burwash from excessive drinking and was buried here by virtue of the coroner's warrant.

Hailsham, 1665
Buried John Lucas, who was smitten with sudden death at the alehouse, having been long tippling there.

Rotherfield, 1843
Buried Thomas Freeman, aged 38, killed by a fall from a rail in drunken frolic.

Some clergymen displayed a decent tolerance of their flock's shortcomings. The 'Handbook for Eastbourne' of 1880, for instance, tells us that 'At Chiddingly all Parish Meetings are held on the Friday before full moon, so that Parishioners attending who may have imbibed too freely will have some chance of reaching their homes safely by the aid of moonlight.'

Remarkably generous. The temptation to point the moral finger was, however, too great for some.

Salehurst, 1610
Henry Turner, a profane drunkard, died excommunicate and was buried in ye highway to the terror of all drunkards.

Sudden Endings

Salehurst, 1808
William Sinden aged 39 buried. Blown into five parts: his head; leg and thigh; body and one leg and thigh; arm; and arm – from the sudden explosion of Brede Gunpowder Mills.

Here we find a parson with an eye for the kind of detail which no newspaper of the time would have had the tastelessness to describe. At least poor Sinden went with such a bang that he surely felt nothing. Compare his fate with the end which befell another, younger William a century earlier. The closet was the pit of a privy, and we have to hope that the fall finished him before he knew where he was.

Westham, 1707
Buried William, son of William & Sarah Weller, aged 14 years, who died by a fall out of a garret into a closet underneath.

The hand of God can occasionally be glimpsed striking down those who trespassed against him.

Hailsham, 1625
Buried Edwarde Willforde, who fell down dead as he was playing a match at football on the Sabbath day.

A good number of deaths have a maritime connection. Sometimes carelessness or human folly plays a part.

Seaford, 1796
Buried John Cosstick, accidentally killed by falling down the cliff, by endeavouring to take mews' eggs.

Tarring Neville, 1763
Buried William Leonard, who broke his bones by falling over the cliff at a wreck.

Drownings often prompted detailed entries in the registers.

Brighton, 1665
The 16th day were lost and drowned at sea in one boat that was dredging for oysters the two Webbs, Ric. Howell Junior, Bestedfast Eliot & the rest, and out of another dredger being overset two more, and they have left behind them 22 fatherless children.

Brighton, 1658
Buried John Comber & a young man who ran into the sea to save one Robert March, a boy who was swimming & cried out 'O save me, I shall be drowned!' and the said Jo. Comber presently ran into the sea & caught the boy by ye hand, but he was drowned.

Rye, 1793
Buried John Hollons and Richard Oke. These young
men, each aged 18 years, were both drowned in
attempting to make the harbour the 1st inst. They
belonged to *The Stag* cutter, Capt. Haddick, & had
been out with seven others in search of smuggling
vessels in one of the said cutter's boats, which by a
sudden gust of wind was overset.

*Two solid round objects are set into the tower of St Clement's
church at Hastings. One is said to be a cannonball fired from
a ship at sea, the other being a matching replica. Not unlikely,
it seems.*

St Clement's, Hastings, 1628
Buried Humphrey Rutland, who was slain in a ship of
Shoreham by a shot at sea from the enemy.

St Clement's, Hastings, 1641
Buried John, a miller, who was killed with a shot from
the sea.

Some corpses had no-one to blame but themselves.

Waldron, 1662
William Dike Gent buried, being shot through the
neck with his own gun, accidentally by his own hand.

Wadhurst, 1805
Buried Sarah Richardson, age 13. Accidentally drowned in a pond at Beggars Bush, the ice breaking under her.

Death By Fish is recorded at Newhaven, though why the parson thought to mention that it was self inflicted is something of a mystery.

Newhaven, 1593
Buried William Picardin, who choked by taking a sole fish, of his own accord, in his mouth.

Sportsmen always run the risk of taking Death's early bath.

Dallington, 1803
Buried John Pinyon, aged 44. Death by wrestling with a person by the name of Dan (at the Horse & Groom at Rushlake Green), who by a trip or kick broke his leg, which brought on a fever that seized his brain.

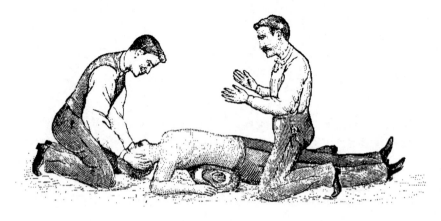

Many 'industrial accidents' are recorded in the Sussex burial registers.

Seaford, 1773
James, son of Joseph and Elizabeth Stevens, killed by a sweep of Mr Washer's windmill.

Bolney, 1832
James Wilmer, aged 30. Crushed in a mill near Cuckfield.

Waldron, 1742
Richard Hickmer, who was killed by a load of faggots running over him.

Withyham, 1775
Francis, son of William and Sarah. Killed on the spot near Wych Cross, the Hartfield carrier's waggon passing over the lower part of his body.

Warbleton, 1722
James Swift, killed by a chalk waggon.

Rusper, 1709
Thomas, son of John Woodman of Beeding, drowned in Warnham Mill pond.

Worth, 1675
**A man drowned in Will Wickenden's marl pit.
Brought to be burying.**

*The man who recorded Thomas Hook's death at Dallington
had the novelist's touch. We're given both detail and drama.*

Dallington, 1803
**Buried Thos. Hook, aged 73. As he was speaking, or
going to speak, to the Heathfield carriers who were
passing his house, he dropped down and died without
a groan.**

And then there were unaccountable Acts of God.

Wadhurst, 1790
Samuel Waller killed by lightning at the Rock.

Uckfield, 1655
**Mr Knelle, the minister of Hartfield, which was killed
in the thunder, was buried the 17th day of July.**

Cocking, 1833
**William Marshall, accidentally killed by the falling in
of a Chalk Pit on Cocking Hill, 61. Supposed to have
been caused by the Earthquake.**

What Did You Call Me?

Wadhurst, 1736
Buried Living, the son of Thomas French.

This apparently monstrous burial at Wadhurst has a simple explanation: young master French had actually been given the Christian name Living. It could have been far, far worse for him. How did poor Fly Fornication Richardson survive the ridicule at Waldron?
During the 17th century, and a little to either side of it, Puritan parents loved to give their offspring names which would be a lifetime's reminder of their duties and sometimes (Godblessing, Safe on Highe) of their extreme good fortune.

We must assume that these afflicted children had ordinary names for day-to-day use, and there's a clue at Shoreham to the compromises that were made.

New Shoreham, 1652
Baptised Thomas, son of Thomas and Faint-not Poole.

A memorial to Faint-not in the church reads:

Here lieth buried Fanny Poole, the wife of Thomas Poole.

Since these Puritan 'handles' were so widespread, we'll content ourselves with a sample drawn from a number of Sussex parishes.

Bethankfull	Muchmarcy
Churchyard	Muchmorefruite
Comfort	No-merit
Craven	Obydeyence
Dedicate	Preserved
Divitmandroit	Refraine
Fleefornication	Rejoyce
Freegift	Repent
Goodgifte	Silence
Lament	Sin-deny
Laud-on-high	Soryforsine
Learnwysdom	Temperance
Morefruite	Thankfull

And see a further example on page 102.

There are, of course, other ways of inflicting shame or ridicule upon our offspring. Parents at Warbleton with the surnames Leafe and Lemon were responsible for these two acts of nomenclatural violence:

Onnion Leafe
Obadiah Orange Lemon

As today, clergymen could sometimes be a little sniffy about registering names they regarded as undignified. Tobias Henshaw, rector of Slinfold from 1672 to 1711, presumably had no quarrel with the weird inventions of God-fearing parents, but he drew the line (or would like to have done) at shortened forms. He couldn't prevent the practice, so he expressed his distaste in the register of baptisms.

Slinfold
February 10, 1696/7 **Naldret, Betty (for soe they would have her named) daughter of Henry & Alice.**

January 31, 1700/1 **Churchar, Harry (for soe they would have him named) sone of Mr Thomas & Mary.**

December 12, 1707 **Farley, Betty (for soe they would have her called) daughter of George & Anne.**

That seeming indecision about the year in the first two entries was commonplace in the old registers, and reflects the long debate in England about changing the calendar. Roman Catholic Europe had long since adopted the Gregorian calendar, which corrected an inaccuracy in computing the length of the year and, at the same time, began each new year on January 1 rather than March 25 as previously. Little Betty Naldret was therefore born in 1696 according to the English system, but in 1697 as far as our continental neighbours were concerned.
    At last we fell into line.

Buxted
1751. N.B. The year 1752 begins with January by Act of Parliament. J.L. Curate

Sometimes a tantalising nickname is used.
Old Primer buried.

The registers also provide an interesting reminder of surnames which have disappeared – often, no doubt, because the ridicule was too much to bear.

Clayton, 1753
Buried George Hedgehog, a gardener.

Preston, Brighton, 1743
Buried Francis son of Benjamin Hogsflesh & Elizabeth his wife.

Hove, 1794
Buried Harriott, daur. of William & Jane Blink.

Children are often named for special reasons which the world at large will never appreciate, so we have to be thankful to vicars who give us fascinating detail.

Fletching, 1791
Baptised Marina, daughter of John and Catherine Maynard. Born on board the Dover packet *The British Fair*, Captain Saunders Commander, on the way from Calais.

Far From Home

Wadhurst, 1698
Buried John Wakeford. This was a disbanded soldier whose orders brought him to Lamberhurst, where he continued from Shrove Sunday till Easter Monday & then, his money failing & his health decaying, he was with threatening driven to shift for himself, & being unable to travel was constrained several  **times to lie down upon the ground in showers of rain & hail between Lamberhurst & Wadhurst, where he soon died.**

Nothing but compassion can have prompted the vicar to tell this story in the register. Strangers were a rarity in rural Sussex in years gone by, when many people travelled a few miles at most from their birthplace, and sometimes these itinerants died not only far from home, but completely unknown.

Cuckfield, 1622
A Bedlam man found dead in Pickwell ground.

Fletching, 1794
Buried a traveller, an American.

Whether known or nameless, this catalogue of men and women who perished while on their travels makes pathetic reading.

Pevensey, 1703
Buried Henry Green, a sailor that belonged to Her Majesty's Ship *Resolution*, which was driven upon this coast in ye late storm and stranded on 27th November last.

Bolney, 1839
Buried Mary Hairs, aged 12. An Irish girl, daughter of a tramper.

A tramper was a tramp or vagrant.

Bolney, 1847
Buried Diana Long, aged 60. A tramper, burned to death.

St Michael, Lewes, 1744
Buried James Scott, a Scotch gardener.

St Clement's, Hastings
Buried James Dunbar of Edinburgh in Scotland, a journeyman tailor.

Cuckfield, 1607
Buried Margerit, a stranger who died at the Lady Bowyer's hay barn.

Warbleton, 1731
Buried a beggar-boy.

*There's a field on Huntons Farm
in Warbleton which is known as
Beggarboys, and local legend
has it that a poor waif died here
alone and unfriended. Was this
the very same lad?*

Warbleton, 1742
Buried a travelling man, his name unknown.

Pevensey, 1708
**Buried Thomas Baker of West Dean, who was found
dead, frozen stiff in ye snow, sitting withinside of ye
Haven wall leading from Pevensea.**

Rusper, 1593
**Buried William Bellingham, a petty chapman &
traveller.**

*The Shorter Oxford English Dictionary gives a 1592
definition of a chapman as 'an itinerant dealer; a hawker,
pedlar'.*

Ticehurst, 1587
**A poor wayfaring man died in a barn at Quedlaye,
buried.**

Ticehurst, 1589
A soldier, a Scottish man died at Flimwell, buried.

Pevensey, 1709
Buried Philip Trouchee (alias in English Trooshe), a prisoner out of France released.

Ashburnham, 1590
John, a straggling soldier, could go no further & was here buried.

Bolney, 1850
Buried Thomas Carter. Found suffocated in the shallow water close to the bridge that crosses the little stream in Buncton Lane. The deceased was a journeyman baker, and had left home four days previously in depressed spirits.

Sexual Peccadilloes

Wadhurst, August 15th, 1784
**Baptised Ann Baldock, base born daughter of Thomas
Baldock, Blacksmith, & Mary Avard,
a noted Strumpet.**

*Nothing seems to have aroused the
clergy's wrath as much as the sexual
irregularities they witnessed all around
them. The vicar who wrote the above
entry found himself having to be even
more emphatic a few months later.*

Wadhurst, December 19, 1784
**Baptised Harriet, base born daughter of Elizabeth
Rogers, a very noted Strumpet of this Parish.**

*The term 'base born' is preferred to 'bastard' by some
clergymen, and BB is found as an acceptable short form in at
least one baptismal register.*

Bolney, 1832
Elizabeth Blaker. Parents: Rebecca. Father's trade: BB.
This is followed by a pencilled note:
by Grinsted, a labourer of Horsham.

Wadhurst, 1647
**Buried Bridget Woodman, who destroyed her baseborn
child.**

Cuckfield, 1619
Baptised Richard, bastard of the widow French, by one Briant as supposed.

Cuckfield, 1675
Baptised Anne, bastard of Elizabeth French & William Boorer, reputed father.

Laughton, 1724
Baptised Thomas, a bastard son of Elizabeth Thatcher.

Worth, 1678
Baptised Elizabeth, daughter of Timothy Blake, widow, no father confessed.

Withyham
Baptised Anne Briseday, base daughter of Elizabeth Hewet and a rascal unknown. Her second bastard.

Occasionally we find a resigned, almost affectionate, note creeping in. Quite what judgement the vicar was making of the parishioner in the following entry we can't be sure, since in the Sussex to fornicate could mean to idle, or dawdle. One guesses, however, that his sins were very much of the flesh.

Ashburnham, 1576
Buried Thomas Winfield, that old fornicator.

Angmering, 1765
Baptised William, son of Anne Robarts by God Knows Who.

Angmering, 1749
Baptised George, son (perhaps) of Richard, certainly of Sarah Amore.

If paternity was often questionable, at other times it was all too apparent.

Fletching
Baptised John, son of John and Mary Huggett.
Baptised William, natural son of Mary Devenish, the aforesaid John being his father.
Memorandum: His wife's son and the son of his concubine were baptised at the same time.

Another unseemly tangle is discovered at Angmering, whose waggish rector, James Croker, we have to thank for three inspired entries on this page.

Angmering, 1757
Baptised James, son of Widow Crossingham, sworn & confessed to have been begotten by her late husband's son. Upon examining the lad, he solemnly declared the hussy attacked him on his bed, first in her clothes, then naked. He did not comply. But afterwards she rushed into his bed naked & seized the premises.

The Shipley register tells the running story of Luke Collison and his housekeeper, Emily Adams.

Shipley 1864
Baptised Henry Collison Adams, son of Emily Adams.

Shipley, 1869
Baptised Mary Ann Collison Adams, daughter of Emily Adams.

Shipley, 1875
Married, Luke Collison and Emily Adams.

The tale of Diana Gaskins (the name, as so often, is irregularly spelt) is far sadder.

Warbleton, 1635
Buried Thomas, son of Dyna Gaskins, a bastard.

Warbleton, 1653
Buried Diana Gasskin, who was born illegitimate and did live upon alms.

The occasional entry makes no secret of the vicar's disgust.

Worth, 1679
Baptised Anne, the base born begotten daughter of John Potter, begotten upon the body of Susan Best.

That kind of clergyman probably rejoiced in the punishment meted out to some sinners.

Pevensey, 1659

Thomas ye son of John and Frances Brooke was baptized the 12th day of June, the said Frances having

been corrected by public whipping in the Liberty of Pevensey, and in the face of the public congregation confessing her sin.

Whether the poor woman's sin involved anything more than having a child out of wedlock is unknown.

The following couple's punishment was attributable not only to their lax morality but to a stroke of sheer bad luck.

Fletching, 1767

Buried Pleasante Sharpe, the concubine of the late Thomas Hall, by whom she had 4 natural children. Pretended to be his wife till a discovery was made by his real wife coming here the very day one of the children was baptised. They both did a public penance for their iniquities.

The Fletching register has its own little soap opera in the eleven years from 1760.

May 31st, 1760
Baptised George, son of Elizabeth Chapman née Holmes. Husband a soldier and abroad with the army, and has been above a year, so the child is not his.

July 27th, 1766
Baptised Edward, son of Thomas Taylor and Elizabeth Chapman née Holmes. Supposed to have another husband living who went for a soldier.

January 15th, 1769
Baptised Elizabeth, daughter of Thomas Taylor and Elizabeth née Holmes.

April 28th, 1771
Baptised Sarah, daughter of Thomas Taylor and Elizabeth Taylor, who as he says is his wife.

It's hard to imagine that anyone was very bothered about a relationship so obviously permanent, but some vicars could never let the chance of censure pass by.

Withyham, 1776
Buried Jane Weller, (Not) the wife (Never married) of Edward. Brought in a waggon, the road being almost impassable by the great weight of snow.

Sometimes, on the other hand, we find a lack of criticism just where we would expect to find it. What was going on here?

Piddinghoe, 1701
Henry, son of James Ford and Grace his niece of the parish of Southease, born April 8th, 1691, baptised November 30th, 1701.

Couples who flouted convention were, of course, strongly encouraged to make amends as quickly as possible, and many did as they were told.

Fletching, 1775
Russell Jarret. Baptised John, natural son of Mary J. and Richard Russell. They married the same day.

We find a string of late marriages in the mid-19th century baptismal register at Bolney, where the vicar, Joseph Dale, was clearly averse to putting a non-commital dash in the space allotted to the father's occupation.

Bolney, 1850
Julia Theresa Hills. Parents: Matilda. Father's trade: single woman. This child was born some weeks before the mother's marriage with the reputed father, John Henty.

Bolney, 1850

George Moore. Parents: Caroline. Father's trade: single woman. Caroline Moore was married this morning.

Bolney, 1851

Barnett, alias Lewry, James. Father's trade: Higler. *N.B.* **The name of Barnett is here placed before that of Lewry, the children being all born before wedlock.**

A higler (or higgler) is glossed in Parish's dialect dictionary as 'A huckster; so called from higgling over his bargains'.

Some people perhaps took the urgings of authority too much to heart. In the records of the Palace Chapter at Chichester we read that no fewer than three marriage licences (involving three different women) were issued to the rather desperate Henry Ide in the space of nine days during April, 1738.

Other folk, of course, should never have married at all.

St Peter the Great, Chichester, 1723

By licence Edward Smith of Warblington and Mary Hammond of Boxgrove. (She, viz M.H. was a great cheat, took a false name, and by that imposed on E. Smith. She had had several bastards.)

Winchelsea, 1806
I, Thomas, am ready to make oath George Loyde
said Ann Mabbs was not his wife because he had
one before. Ann Mabbs also asserts that he (very
graciously) told her as much immediately after their
marriage.

Brighton, 1655
The contract & purpose of marriage between James
Bishopp & Margaret Grimell, both of this town, was
published, & upon the second publishing thereof
came in Richard Baker of Stanmer and forbade it,
& I asked him what he could object against it, and he
answered she was his wife by promise.

*In view of all these shenanigans we have to feel sorry for the
Greenfields (were they perhaps cousins?), a couple who
wanted to marry but were refused permission.*

Billingshurst, 1762
Banns read between Richard Greenfield, widower,
and Mary Greenfield, both of Billingshurst. Forbid by
the Governor of the workhouse. His reasons are
inability to maintain a wife as he is, or has been for
several years, maintained by this parish on account of
old age etc.

Most of us like to cut a bit of a dash at our weddings, and some of those who tied the knot in ages past would have been shocked to read the notes entered by their vicar in the register.

West Hoathly, 1714
Married Wm Mason and Ann Young, an old widow.

After such heartless stuff, it's a pleasure to end this section with a touching, if sad, farewell which has not the slightest suggestion of the censorious or deflating about it.

Herstmonceux, 1540
Buried Alse, the love of John Afford.

Foul Deeds

Harting, 1601
This year about the feast day of St Michael
the Archangel, or shortly after, the bones
and apparel of John Roche was found in
Halewood within the parish of Harting
(which John Roche was suspected to have
been killed there by William Tormer, who
was hanged at the next assize at East
Grinstead for the same fact and other robberies). Also
the said bones buried in the place where they were
found, by the appointment of the coroner.

*Murders and suspected murders make several appearances in
the Sussex parish registers. Some vicars give us the details,
while others leave us longing to know what happened next.*

Brightling, 1776
**Buried Joseph Cruttenden. He was murdered by his
wife, who was tried and condemned to death at the
following assizes at Horsham, and burnt.**

*Poor Joseph had married his wife Ann when he was 35 and
she was in her seventies. An inquest jury found that 'seduced
by the instigation of the Devil', he stabbed him 'with a knife of
the value of two pence'.*

St Peter the Great, Chichester
Buried Thos. Belton, (who died) by eating arsenic in bread and butter, West Street, from Mr Barnaby's public house. Age 61.

Worth, 1689
Buried Francis Swifte. Supposed to be murdered by his father.

Brighton, 1646
Buried Richard Hames, being shot in the powle by Jo. Snooke with a fowling piece.

The 'powle' was presumably Richard's 'poll', or head.

Warbleton, 1573
Buried Tomson Fawterell and Ellinor Fawterell, who were most cruelly murdered by one Thomas Homan, apprentice with Richard Taylor of Heathfield, upon a Sabbath day in the morning prayer, while in the house of Thomas Fawterell, father to the said Tomson and brother of Ellinor, whose confession was that he came to steal money to play at cards and dice.

Chailey, 1594
Buried Thomas Beard, that was secretly murdered, the doer thereof yet unknown.

Brightling, 1750
Buried Thos. Boden, a soldier who was murdered in a quarrel.

Mayfield, 1853
Pharas Androv, supposed to have been starved in the house of John Banks, was, after the sitting of Mr Fowl the coroner upon him, buried.

A strange name, and an uncertain death. To 'starve' in early times sometimes meant to die from hunger, cold, grief or slow disease, although the wording here does suggest that poor Pharas was bumped off.

Suicide is less often mentioned in the registers, and is sometimes only implied.

Worth, 1662
Alice Taylor drowned. Was buried without solemnity.

This is a reminder that suicide was regarded as a mortal sin, denying the perpetrator a decent burial.

Ore, 1616

Buried in the highway near Fareligh Towne end Richard Andrews, who hanged himself in his own house.

Harting, 1610

John Mowdye of Dicham in the parish of Harting hanged himself, and was buried aside of hemnere in Harting between two lordships in the highway the first day of June by the appointment of the coroner.

Hemner Hill lies due west of South Harting church. The 'lordships' were manors, so that the unhappy John was buried in no-man's land.

In one entry Latin obscures the deed.

Ticehurst, 1729

Lunatica quae sese suffocavit aquis. (A mad woman who drowned herself).

While perhaps the most terrible entry is at Hastings.

St Clement's, Hastings, 1817
Buried Richard Harlot, 63, a razor grinder – cut his own throat.

Little Children

Shipley, 1708
All born at one birth, 2 Feb, George, Joane, Mary, Elizabeth, children of John King by Jane his wife, were baptised 3 Feb and all buried in one coffin 8 Feb.

If life was often short in earlier times, those who survived were often part of uncomfortably large families. The following would surely have made it into a contemporary Guinness Book of Records.

Laughton, 1794
A few days since, the wife of a labouring man of Laughton near the town (Lewes) named Goldsmith was safely delivered of her 25th child.

Other entries are even more amazing, to the point of being, alas, unbelievable.

Wadhurst, 1691
Baptised Elizabeth, daughter of Francis and Ann Comber. This child was heard crying in the womb before it was born.

Sometimes the newcomers were regarded as a great nuisance by parish ratepayers who had no option but to support them.

Pyecombe, 1730
Jane, daughter of Jane Drudge, an interloper who was forced upon this parish, baptised.

Fletching, 1755
Baptised William, son of John and Elizabeth Wood. John Wood has sworn himself upon the parish, but I believe falsely. He is a bad man.

Fletching, 1723
Baptised Joseph, a child left on a Sunday near the church.

Fletching, 1728
Baptised Susannah, a poor child born in a barn.

The death of a child is always painful to read – especially when it follows a happier entry in the register.

Stanmer, 1664
Sybilla Cooter, ye daughter of Edward Cooter and Elizabeth his wife, was baptised ye 19th day of February.

Stanmer, 1665
Sybilla Cooter, ye daughter of Edward Cooter and Elizabeth his wife, was buried ye 6th day of January - burned by a fall into ye fire, whereof it died.

Brighton, 1655
Buried John, son of John Pokocke, who was drowned in a little water.

Brighton, 1657
The ninth, buried Alice, daughter of Mr Stephen Ramesden, a leprous maiden.

Some little mites were unworthy of a decent send-off.

Bolney, 1839
Martha Lindfield, an infant. Unbaptised, and buried without the funeral service.

But the vicar might still show mercy.

Falmer, about 1800
The child was unbaptised, but a short service was held by me at the graveside.

Many children died from diseases and ailments which would have been treatable today - and endured their suffering for much longer.

Hellingly, 1811
Buried Christopher Curtis, aged 7. This child was an object of real pity. It had from a quarter year old been afflicted with dropsy of the brain, the head a yard in circumference and produced when dead 7½ pints of water.

Then, as now, some feckless parents could have done more for their offspring.

Bolney, 1849
Buried Elizabeth Genden, age 12. On inquest verdict, died of scarlet fever and neglect of parents and exposure to cold.

Neglect, of course, takes various guises.

Cocking, 1799
Buried the d. of John & Ann Kingshot. Thro' the shameful neglect of the Parents never was baptized, they being Methodist, presume, contrary to the express injunction of our Saviour, not to hold with baptism.

Perhaps the most prestigious christening enjoyed by the parents of a new-born child occurred at Rye.

Rye, 1725
Baptised George, son of James Lamb, Mayor, and Martha, his wife.
    ***Memorandum* - that King George landed at Rye on Monday ye 3rd of January, being driven into our bay by a storm in his return from Hanover, and stayed here till Friday ye 7th of January, & he stood Godfather for Mr Lamb's child ye 5th.**

A Day's Work

Wadhurst, 1638
Buried Thos. Upton the Archimedes of Wadhurst. This was by trade glover, joiner, carpenter, instrument maker, curious workman for jacks, clocks, stoves and vices for glaziers.

The parish registers offer riches to researchers of all kinds. We've already made the acquaintance of a higler, and many another occupation makes an appearance. Here's a brief selection.

St Michael, Lewes, 1759
Buried Charles Hood, drummer of the marines.

West Hoathly, 1760
Buried John Parkhurst, age 88, who was a soldier under Marlborough.

Ticehurst, 1585
Thomas Slye, the kitchen boy of my Lady Hendleye, buried.

Burwash, 1761
Buried William Kent, the Lewes News carrier.

Rotherfield, 1768
Buried a travelling man, a viper catcher.

Ashburnham, 1652
Buried John Thomas, the bonesetter.

Stanmer, 1639
Buried an old bellows mender called Hobs, a waygoer.

Millers were proverbial cheats, so it's heartening to know that the slur was sometimes unjustified.

Ashburnham, 1637
Solomon Southernden (an honest miller) was buried (to the great loss and grief of all his customers).

Whereas, in sharp contrast, here's an 'occupation' that would have been kept rather quiet in the man's lifetime.

Burwash, 1803
Buried Thomas Waterhouse, aged 35 (a smuggler).

Miscellaneous

Withyham, 1780
Mr Davies baptised someone he could not recollect.

Our assemblage of this-and-thats begins with an entry presumably written by a clerk unable to get any sense out of his parson - and not prepared to enquire further.
    What a contrast with the following, entered by a town clerk and registrar who, sadly, knew the identity of the person in question only too well.

Brighton, October 1664
The first day was buried Elizabeth, the wife of me, Adam Cartwright, who had been married together 50 years.

With life often short, vicars were sometimes sufficiently impressed by longevity to make a note of it.

Cuckfield, 1797
Buried John Ellis, who within a few months of his death walked one day to Lewes, and the next continued his journey to Seaford. Aged 97.

Chailey, 1602
Buried Marian Coston, *anno aetatis suae circiter centesimo*. (Aged about a hundred years.)

Not all claims, however, were completely trustworthy.

Wadhurst, 1683
Old Peter Sparks of Salehurst buried. Above 126 years old by his own computation.

Outbreaks of disease being commonplace, we find many references to them, although often without much clue as to their nature.

Fletching, 1582
The names of such as were suspected today of the plague. First a stranger died, and was buried upon the common of Piltdown.
    One of Nicholas Holfor's children was buried on the same common.

Hailsham, 1699
All those that died of the smallpox had no affidavits, so I suppose they were buried in woollen.

There are many references in the registers to the dead being buried in woollen shrouds. An act of 1666 (not repealed until 1814) stipulated that everyone should be buried in this humble fashion, so boosting the wool trade. There was a way out for the wealthy, however: they could bury their dead in linen if they paid a fine, as one of the Pelhams seems belatedly to have done.

Laughton, 1681

Mrs Elizabeth Pelham, the wife of Thomas Pelham Esq, was buried on the 13th day of October.

Mem. That on the 21st I certified John Shoesmith and John Barnard, Overseers of the Poor for Laughton, that there is no affidavit and certificate brought to me within eight days (the limit for the act) concerning the said corpse of Mrs Elizabeth Pelham, interred and buried in woollen according to a late Act of Parliament Instituted, an Act for Burying in Woollen.

Sir John Pelham gave £20 for the poor of the parish.

A happy conclusion all round, but many an inglorious end is recorded in the registers.

Fletching, 1651

Buried Richard Tomsett, who died in the fields.

Stanmer, 1673

John Whitebread was buried ye 13th day of July. He died intestate, because he had nothing to bequeath.

Brighton, 1641

Robert Kenward was put in the ground & no burial.

Gravestones were to become a churchyard feature only from the late seventeenth century, but Robert's stark dispatch must have been especially minimal to merit a mention in the register.

An angrily sarcastic response to the disrespectful treatment of the dead is to be found at Pevensey. The town was administered by a body called the Jurat.

Pevensey, 1773
The body of a man drowned at sea was buried naked in the beach because Mr John Breden the then bailiff would not permit the person who found it to bring it up to be buried in the churchyard. The Minister desired to have it brought up & he would bury it without any fees, but the HUMANE Jurat forbad it.

Some vicars were unable to resist the moralising note. In some cases, to be fair, they were prompted by truly wretched circumstances.

Arlington, 1613
Baptised Stephen, the son of John Williams, executed a fortnight before for stealing. God give his son more grace.

Arlington, 1615
Buried Stephen, the son of John Williams executed for felony. *Deus Cui Vult Miseretur.* (God pardons whom he pleases.)

Mistakes have always been liable to happen, although they are not always recorded with the frankness of the following entry.

Brighton, 1843
Buried Mary Ann Parsons, aged 31, from the hospital. This body was buried June 17th, the coffin having been buried without the body on June 14th by some mistake of the porter at the hospital.

Among the choicest curiosities is a pair of entries at Slaugham. The first has a slightly pompous ring.

Slaugham, March 3rd 1800
On the above day a yew tree was planted in the churchyard at Slaugham in line with the southwest corner of the church by the Reverend D. Pape, Rector; Mr James Langly, Churchwarden; Mr John Lindfield, Parish Clerk. Railed in by Thomas Hearsey, Carpenter.

Whoever followed this up three years later was clearly no friend of the churchwarden or the carpenter – the latter, if the entry is accurate, a less than competent craftsman. Presumably, with his command of Latin, the writer was the successor of, or a stand-in for, Mr Pape. Did he perhaps resent his posting to the Sussex Weald?

Slaugham, April 17th 1803
Mala ave, for the yew tree is dead, the railing is decayed, the rector is gone, the churchwarden is not, the carpenter is not and the parish clerk is away. *Sic transit gloria mundi. Memor esto brevis cor.* (So fades the world's glory. Take this transience to heart.)

Since the frailties of human nature are so commonly on view in the parish registers, it's a rare pleasure to discover praise being lavished on the few – even if, in the first two cases, we note that the vicar's encomia were very much 'in house'.

Steyning, 1613
Buried Elizabeth, wife of John Michaell, Clerk, a virtuous matron and of worthy stock descended.

Steyning, 1615
Mrs Anne Michaell, widow, a virtuous and godly matron, having lived (with Anna) a holy life, and dying (with Job) old and full of days, was buried (with Abraham) in a good age.

Lancing, 1691
John Wolven, commonly called the honest man, buried June 13th.

Slinfold, 1580
Buried Mary Pendfold, daughter of Richard, having now accomplished 24 years of age, for whose death, by reason of her virtuous life, were lamenting tears of young and old.

There's a mystery about an entry at Ore, which predates the founding of the Society of Friends (or Quakers) by some twenty years. Which organisation, then, can this be?

Ore, 1625
Buried Mr John Crispe Esquire, not by the minister of the parish, but by the Company of Friends about with tapers and other ceremonies of their own possession.

Church congregations were often prompted, as part of a national effort, to give money to a good cause. Their generosity or otherwise is sometimes recorded.

Arlington, 1692
September ye 12th. Collected in this Parish by virtue of a brief for the redemption of the slaves in Turkey, Sarjear and suchlike places £1.2s.0d.

Laughton, 1630
Collected in the parish of Laughton towards the relief of the inhabitants of the maritime town of Southwold in the county of Essex the sum of ten shillings and two pence.

Laughton, 1631
Collected in the parish of Laughton towards the relief of the distressed inhabitants of Ilminster the sum of five shillings, ten pence.

Some entries are unclassifiably odd.

Bolney, 1850
The remains of the late Lady Oakeley interred with the understanding that her relatives have permission to remove the same at any future time.

Jevington, 1874
Married Thomas Leonard Pierce, aged 26, and Charlotte Elizabeth Wickerson, aged 28. The female in this marriage was without arms. The ring was put (& there held by the man) on the 4th toe of the left foot. Her signature was easily & quickly written with her right foot.

Chichester, St Peter the Great 1787
Tho. Peacock buried in Paradise.

The above is not as strange as it appears once you know that the graveyard outside Chichester Cathedral was known as Paradise. The following, on the other hand, is wonderfully cranky.

Buxted, 1666
Richard Bassett, the old Clerk of this parish who had continued in the offices of Clerk & Sexton in this Parish by the space of 43 years, whose melody warbled forth as if he had been thumped on the back with a stone, was buried the 20th day of September.

And then there were the pew disputes. In times gone by these were often as furious, and as nonsensical to outsiders, as modern arguments between neighbours over walls and fences.

At Ditchling, for instance, the vicar married a widow who, after his death in the early 1600s, gave the archdeacon no end of trouble by refusing to vacate the vicarage pew. At Horsham in the early 19th century there were two notable cases, one featuring a never-say-die character who fixed a plate saying 'Charles Oakes 1 seat' to the contentious pew and kept replacing it each time it was taken down.

The incumbent at Woodmancote, near Henfield, devoted pages to this kind of cantankerousness, which was also an issue at Worth.

Worth, 1632
That the first seat on the right hand next unto the pulpit and on the south side be and hath been belonging time out of mind unto Edward Blunden and his house, called by the name of Shepherds in the Hollow in the parish of Worth, and unto others his Christian fellows, namely Thomas Nicholas, Henry Munche and the Laye House, and unto no other.

The reason of this record is because there have been some alteration and addition unto the said which might breed a question. In witness therefore we have subscribed the day and year above written. Nicholas Whishton, Rector.

We end our collection at Worth, and with a couple of entries which underline the liberties clergymen and their clerks would often take with the parish registers – and which are expressly forbidden today. On the page for 1640 we find:

Mr William Palmer if he had 1000 a year and if he will give me 5 hundred and I would not care.

Quite what this signifies it is impossible to say but it doesn't go unanswered. Further down, someone has added in a different hand:

And then we should be pretty fellows.

Acknowledgements

This book would have been impossible to compile without the generous help of people who had examined their own parish registers or read their local histories and were prepared to pass the fruits of that research on to me.

Although some of their contributions were not strictly relevant to the project I had in mind, they all gave me a great deal of entertainment, and I have included as many as possible.

My thanks to: Fred Avery, Brenda Barton, Joan Black, Alan Boden, Margaret Burgess, Diana Chatwin, Dr Richard Coates, Susan Djabri, José Loosemore, Gwyn Mansfield, David Morris, Mike Parcell, Audrey Rowe, Maurice Thornton, June Walker and Doris Williams.

Further reading

A number of the Sussex parish registers have been published and can be found on the shelves of the reference libraries. Here you should also come across bound copies of the *Sussex Genealogist and Local Historian* and the *Sussex Family Historian*, whose pages are littered with colourful extracts. The many fascinating publications of the Sussex Record Society include transcripts of church 'presentments' - complaints against the ungodly often similar to those found in these pages, but of a formal and public nature.

For an interesting overview of the subject (with a few Sussex references) see W.E. Tate's *The Parish Chest*.

Taking liberties

A difficult decision had to be taken over the presentation of the material in this book, and I have no doubt that purists will be unhappy with the outcome.

The spelling in many of the registers is so erratic (my favourite being 'acceqwecyon' for 'execution' at Rye), that a faithful transcription of them would have necessitated a veritable shower of ultimately tiresome footnotes. I have generally left names as they appear, and the archaic 'ye' for 'the' survives as a reminder that we are dealing with old manuscripts, but otherwise I have used the modern forms throughout.

I have taken another liberty, too. Many of the extracts begin with a 'Baptised', 'Buried' or 'Married' which are not to be found in the original for the very good reason that their appearance under the appropriate heading in the register rendered the wording unnecessary. My priority has been to achieve a comfortable readability.

Serious researchers, then, must go to the registers themselves. I trust (though I admit to relying on the scholarship of my contributors) that they will otherwise find things very much as they are recorded here, and that they will agree that, however presented, the scribblings of our Sussex vicars are an idiosyncratic delight.

Index
of subjects and places